11/15

MASON JAR *Gifts*

Create Heartwarming Gifts Using Canning Jars

Marie Browning

LARK

New York

LARK
New York

An Imprint of Sterling Publishing
1166 Avenue of the Americas
New York, NY 10036

ISBN 978-1-4547-0921-3

Distributed in Canada by Sterling Publishing
c/o Canadian Manda Group, 664 Annette Street
Toronto, Ontario, Canada M6S 2C8
Distributed in the United Kingdom by GMC Distribution Services
Castle Place, 166 High Street, Lewes, East Sussex, England BN7 1XU
Distributed in Australia by Capricorn Link (Australia) Pty. Ltd.
P.O. Box 704, Windsor, NSW 2756, Australia

For information about custom editions, special sales, and premium and corporate purchases,
please contact Sterling Special Sales at 800-805-5489 or specialsales@sterlingpublishing.com.

Manufactured in China

2 4 6 8 10 9 7 5 3 1

larkcrafts.com

CONTENTS

Introduction 6

Canning Jars: A Timeless Product 7

Painted Jars 10
Products 12
Techniques 14
Projects 19
Twenty projects featuring a variety of techniques such as distressing, stenciling, making dots and stripes, faux mercury glass, design painting

Découpage and Trimmed Jars 40
Products 42
Techniques 43
Projects 44
Twelve projects for gluing and sealing a variety of papers to create canisters, votive holders, storage jars, and memory jars

Quick Tricks 60
Twenty-five projects with instructions to make fun and easy items such as drinking mugs, soap dispensers, potpourri jars, votive candleholders, storage jars, coasters, yarn dispensers, and snow globes

Labels and Tags 94

Culinary Gifts 96
Techniques 97
Recipes 98
Sixty-three recipes for making mixes to fill jars plus recipes for making salad dressings, meat dishes, soups, breads, cookies, cakes, chocolate treats, drinks, and doggy treats

Index 126

About the Author 128

Acknowledgments 128

Create heartwarming gifts by decorating plain jars and filling them with offerings of love.

Gifts made with love delight the recipient and reward the giver. The projects you make with the ideas presented here will be much more than handmade jars of culinary treats and practical gifts—they will be gifts of your time, thoughtfulness, and creativity. When handmade gifts are packaged in decorated jars, the containers also become gifts that can be used as storage, a lamp base, a candleholder, or a decorative accessory.

This book contains instructions for making more than 70 beautiful decorated jars, as well as ideas and recipes to spur your own creativity to create hundreds of heartfelt gifts. Some of the projects require planning ahead; others are quick and easy. Not only will you get ideas for filling the jars with culinary delights and other offerings, but also you will learn creative ways to decorate the jars. Techniques such as decoupage, painting, stenciling, and embellishing with notions will make your jars look special. I will show you exciting ways to finish the lids, and then make clever gift cards to go with them.

Celebrate your creativity with special gifts that express you and that are personalized to the gift recipient. While one person would enjoy relaxing bath salts, another would love a jar of homemade snacks. Make each decorated jar a most personal greeting and a wonderful expression of you. Here I've included projects that make perfect holiday gifts for festive winter celebrations as well as projects that are great for giving all year long. Use an everyday happening as a reason to give a gift in a jar—welcome to the neighborhood; thanks for dinner; congratulations on your retirement; I love you. Enter the exciting world of creating and the thrill of giving of one's self. Gifts that are made with the hands and given from the heart are always appreciated and treasured. The cliché, "It's the thought that counts" is true! Most of all have fun!

Canning Jars | A TIMELESS PRODUCT

As far back in time as the ancient Egyptians, glass jars and bottles have been used as containers. The use of glass as a container for preserving food is, however, quite recent. In 1795, a Frenchman, Nicholas Appert invented the process of applying heat to kill bacteria and removing oxygen from jars to prevent the food from deteriorating. Appert, a chef, was determined to win the prize of 12,000 francs offered by Napoleon for a way to prevent military food supplies from spoiling. The first process involved garden peas preserved in champagne bottles. It was a French military secret but soon was leaked to the English. By 1810 an Englishman, Peter Durance, had patented the use of metal containers for canning and was soon opening factories. By the 1860s, canned foods were commonplace.

The major companies that manufacture canning jars today—Ball, Mason, and Kerr—were all started just over 100 years ago. The Ball brothers, Frank and Edmund, founded the Ball Corporation in 1880. They started with a wood-jacketed tin container for paint and varnish and soon expanded into the home-canning field. Ball still produces glass canning jars as well as space systems and electro-optic materials.

Jars used for home canning are often referred to as "Mason" jars after John L. Mason, inventor of the first common canning jar. Mason's patent expired in 1875. Since then, all canning jars are generally called mason jars. The first mason jars were made of blue-green glass. The originals are collectible and quite valuable. The Kerr Company, founded in 1902, developed the two-piece lid, which is comprised of a flat seal and a separate screw-on band. This type of lid is still used today by home canners.

The beauty of glass jars is that they are completely recyclable, inexpensive, and readily available. They are the perfect, inexpensive "blank canvas" for decorating and giving of gifts. There is an almost endless supply of jar types that can be used for your decorative projects. While canning-type jars are the most popular and can be readily purchased at most grocery stores, you can also recycle pickle jars or others types of glass jars from the foods you purchase. Craft stores and container stores also have unique jars that will make your gift-giving special.

MASON-STYLE CANNING JARS

Mason jars are glass jars available in half-pint, pint, quart, and half gallon sizes with standard or wide openings, which are called the "mouth" of the jar. The glass of the jar may be molded or embossed with fruit motifs, diamond patterns, or company names and crests. Also available are blank, un-embossed jars for creative use. You can now find vintage reproduction jars in different colors, shapes, and sizes. Generally, less elaborate jars are used for the projects in this book, but fancier embossed jars can be substituted.

WIRE BAIL JARS

These jars, with glass lids that are held in place with a wire clamp cost a little more but give the finished project a more sophisticated appearance. Made in many sizes and shapes, they can be found at quality kitchen stores and department stores.

DECORATIVE JARS

Many sizes, styles, and shapes of decorative jars are available. Look for seasonal-shaped candy and cookie jars, interesting shapes, and different colors of glass. These types of jars can be found at crafts, kitchen supply, and container stores and gift shops.

RECYCLED JARS

Many jars can be recycled and used again for gift giving. Carefully soak the jars to remove labels and clean them thoroughly. You can save jars all year and be ready with a nice selection whenever you wish to create a gift. Lids with printing can be covered with spray paint, metal paint, or fabric. Recycled jars should **not** be used for canning foods.

ANTIQUE JARS

Antique glass jars are beautiful but their glass is more brittle so they are easier to break. When using older jars, be sure they are free of chips and imperfections. If you are not sure of the value of an old jar, it may be wiser not to use it. The price antique jars have brought is amazing. Some early colored-glass canning jars have been priced at up to $1,000 each! One option is to seek reproductions.

JAR LIDS

Typical canning jar lids come in two parts; a flat metal seal and a screw-on band called a ring. Some older jars have metal screw-on bands and flat glass tops. Still others have glass-lined zinc lids. **Note: When planning to heat process your food for preserving, always use new jars and new seals. Rings can be reused after sanitizing.**

Lid Options:

- Plastic screw-top lids that fit regular canning jars can be purchased. They should be used for short-term food storage and for decoration only.
- One-piece metal screw-top lids (generally used by food manufacturers) can be reused when a seal is not required.
- Glass tops with bail-wire clamps (some with rubber gaskets) make attractive coverings.
- Wooden stoppers with rubber seals are a nice surface for decorating.
- Natural corks are another attractive way to secure the contents of a jar.
- Perforated metal lids for fragrance gifts are available in craft shops or make your own.
- Lids with hanging chains designed to fit regular canning jars are available in craft shops.
- Jars are an excellent base for a candle or lamp. Available at most craft stores are lamp fixtures that screw right onto canning jars in place of the lid.
- Also available are lid lamp kits that allow you to use a decorated jar as an oil lamp. The screw-on lid has a hole in which a glass vial fits. A stopper placed on the vial holds a wick. The glass vial can be filled with lamp oil.

For safety's sake, always give instructions for the use of your lighted jar gift and remind the recipient to never leave a burning candle unattended.

CLEANING YOUR JARS AND LIDS

Clean jars inside and outside with hot soapy water before using or storing. To remove labels or price stickers, soak the jars in hot soapy water for 30 minutes, then peel or rub off labels. Remove the sticky residue left by stickers with a product designed for that purpose. You can make your own residue remover by mixing a solution of 80% alcohol and 20% orange label remover in a spray bottle. This solution will not leave an oily finish. When you are ready to decorate the jar, rub the outside with a soft, lint-free rag and rubbing alcohol to remove all surface grease and fingerprints.

Note: When using food, follow the directions for sterilizing and cleaning jars in the "Culinary Gifts" section.

When reusing metal lids, you can remove labels and printing by spraying the 80/20-alcohol/orange label-remover solution onto the top of the lid. Let it sit for about 10 minutes, then wipe away the label and sticky adhesive with a paper towel. With steel wool, remove any printing with a circular scrubbing motion. Clean the surface with rubbing alcohol before adding your own label or decoration.

Painted Jars

PRODUCTS, TECHNIQUES, AND PROJECTS

There are a variety of painting techniques and types of paints that can be used to beautify your jars. Choosing the right paint is important to create a jar that is lasting. This chapter will give you all the information you need concerning the range of products available, and techniques for decorating with these products.

Even though it seems quite simple, the question most often asked is "What paint do I use on this surface?" Here's the rule: Always select paint intended for use on the surface you are decorating. Read the label on the paint container to determine the paint's compatibility with your surface. This rule goes for painting on glass or on metal lids. For example, if you use acrylic craft paints for painting on glass, the paint will rub off when handled and not be permanent. However, if you use acrylic *glass* paints, your design will be permanent and will not chip or wash off when fully cured.

Today we are fortunate to be able to choose from a wide variety of paints suitable for painting on glass. They offer transparent or opaque coverage and come in a wide range of colors. Many manufacturers have recognized the popularity of painting on glass and have developed paints specifically for that purpose. There are several brands of paint available in each category.

PAINT CAUTIONS

Always follow the paint manufacturer's directions carefully. Do not assume all glass paints are the same.

It is not a good idea to mix different manufacturers' products; e.g., don't use a paint color from Company A and a topcoat from Company B. Each company carefully formulates its paints, mediums, primers, and topcoats to work best together and cannot guarantee results when its products are used with other companies' products.

Pictured are five jars showing a variety of painting techniques that will be explained on the following pages. Moving from left to right: the first jar shows the popular Ombré painting technique that has a variegated look; the jar with the large dots illustrates the technique of stamping dots with a round sponge applicator; the next jar shows a distressing technique; the small dots on the next jar were done with an all-over dot stencil; and the last jar with the hobnail effect was done using dimensional paint dots painted over with an opaque coat.

PAINT PRODUCTS

TRANSPARENT PAINTS

This type of transparent acrylic paint designed for glass is often used to resemble stained glass. For best results when applying the paint, squeeze the paint from the bottle directly onto the surface of the jar. In some cases it can be brushed onto the surface. These types of paints are not washable so should be used for decorative purposes only such as for candle jars. This type of paint is not recommended for use with culinary products.

ACRYLIC ENAMEL PAINTS

These are durable, opaque, high-gloss acrylic paints for glass and offer a wide variety of premixed colors in convenient-sized bottles. Do not thin paints with water. If thinning is needed, use blending mediums or thinning mediums manufactured for that brand of paint. While still wet, the paints clean up easily with soap and water. Choose from opaque colors or frost, transparent, glitter, and specialty finishes such as chalky and chalkboard finish.

These types of paints can be baked in a home oven to make them more durable and washable. (Check labels to see if this is possible with the paint you have chosen.) To bake, let paint dry a full 48 hours. Place the glass jar in a conventional oven (not preheated) and heat to 325 degrees. Bake for 10 minutes. Turn off the oven and allow jar to cool before removing. After baking, painted jars can be hand washed. Some are even okay in the dishwasher!

DIMENSIONAL OUTLINE ACRYLIC ENAMELS

The dimensional type that is squeezed directly from the bottle to the surface and the brush-on type are both great for using on glass jars. The dimensional type is especially effective for special effects like wording or the faux milk-glass technique. They are so easy to use—like holding a pen.

PAINT PENS

Colorful selections of paint pens are available for painting on glass. They are great for detailing and for simple jar decoration without the fuss of brushes. Paint pens come in many colors and in fine, medium, and calligraphy chisel-point tips. Be sure the paint pens you choose are recommended for glass.

SPRAY PAINTS

Spray paint is a very fast and effective way to add a painted surface to the outside or inside of a jar. New finishes such as mirror, chalk, and transparent easily transform your jars into beautiful pieces. These paints are not meant to be used when placing food inside. They are not permanent, and the jars cannot be washed.

PAINT APPLICATORS

You will need a variety of good quality artist's brushes.
- $1/2$" and 1" flat glaze brushes for basecoating and painting large motifs
- #1 and #4 round brushes for general painting and details
- #0 and #00 liners for fine detailing
- Stencil brushes
- Round shaped sponges for stenciling and adding dotted patterns.
- Dense foam sponges (the type used for applying makeup), for stenciling and edging

OTHER SUPPLIES

- Freezer paper for cutting stencils, protecting your work surface, or as a paint palette
- Wax paper to use as a palette
- Sanding block or emery board
- Baby wipes
- Cotton swaps
- Small disposable containers
- Rubbing alcohol
- Paper towels for cleanup
- Water basin for rinsing and cleaning brushes
- Masking tape
- Transfer paper and a stylus for transferring patterns to the outside of jar
- Brush-cleaning soap for brush care

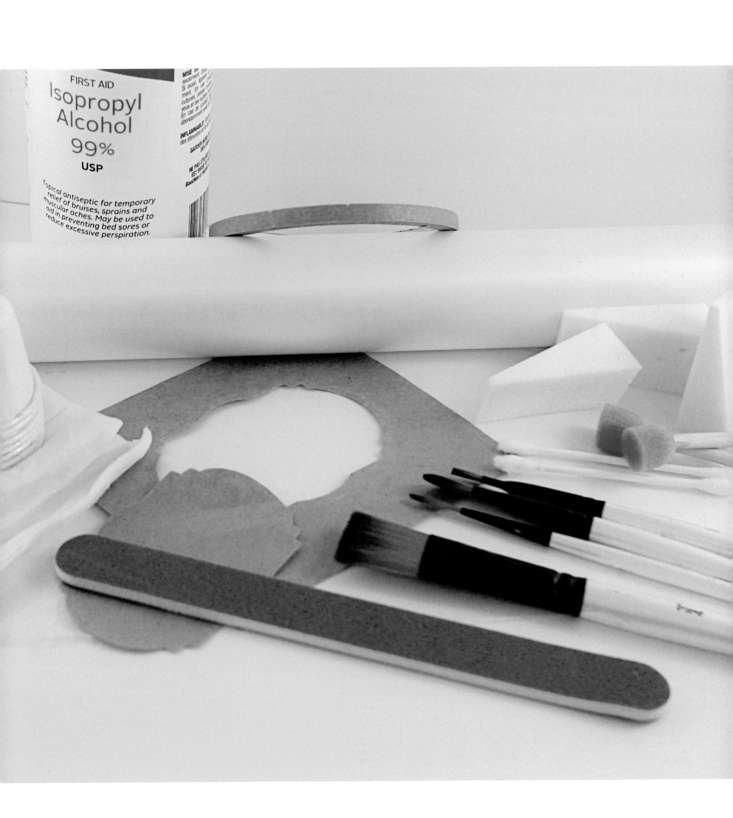

FIRST AID
Isopropyl
Alcohol
99%
USP

Topical antiseptic for temporary
relief of bruises, sprains and
muscular aches. May be used to
aid in preventing bed sores or
reduce excessive perspiration.

PAINTING TECHNIQUES

SURFACE PREPARATION

Thoroughly clean and dry jars before applying paint. Rub the surface well with rubbing alcohol, holding the jar by the neck to avoid fingerprints. When using paints specifically manufactured for painting on glass, follow the paint manufacturer's directions carefully for preparing the glass surface.

TRANSFERRING DESIGNS

For transparent jars that do not have a basecoated surface, place a photocopy of the pattern inside the jar. Use a small piece of tape inside the jar to hold the pattern in place and put two or three crumpled paper towels in the jar to hold the pattern against the inside of the jar. (This is easier than taping all around the pattern to hold it flat against the glass.)

For jars that have been painted with an opaque basecoat, use wax-free colored transfer paper such as red or blue, which is easier to see on the glass surface. Carefully tape the transfer paper in place over the jar, making sure the paper is right-side down. Tape pattern in place atop transfer paper. With a stylus, trace the pattern firmly to transfer the design to the jar.

BASECOATING

Using a Brush: For full, opaque coverage using brush-on paint, apply it with a fairly heavy application—heavy enough so it coats the glass but not so heavy that the paint drips and sags. Two or three coats are usually needed; be sure to let the paint dry fully between coats.

Using a Sponge: Apply the paint by stippling with a sea sponge. Make sure the sponge is damp and all excess water has been squeezed out. Dip the sponge into the paint and apply to the jar in an up and down dabbing motion. Apply two or three coats and let each coat dry fully. This technique gives the surface a slight texture.

Using Spray Paint: First protect your workspace with newspaper and work in a well-ventilated, warm area. Prop the jar up with an upended disposable container on the work surface. Shake the can well. For outsides of jars, spray three to four light coats, working 12" away from the jar. Let each coat dry thoroughly to avoid runs and over spraying. For the insides of jars, use masking tape to secure a protective piece of freezer paper on the outside of jar, beginning at the mouth of the jar. Spray with small bursts into the the jar making sure not to overspray. The drying time between coats may take a bit longer.

CLEANING EDGES

Painting near the neck of the jar is sometimes tricky. Use a

Pattern is placed inside a clear jar.

Tape transfer paper and pattern to jar.

This shows transferred pattern on basecoated jar.

slightly dampened cotton swab on the wet paint to clean this top edge perfectly.

Cleaning neck with cotton swab

USING MASKING TAPE FOR STRAIGHT EDGES

Masking tape is the perfect solution when you want straight edges or perfect stripes. Place the tape over the areas where you want no paint. A ruler is handy to use as a guide for placing the tape. Rub tape to adequately adhere edges to avoid run-unders. Apply paint with a brush or a sponge. Allow paint to dry thoroughly before removing the tape. Use a sharp art knife to cut along the edge of the masking tape, cutting into the paint for perfect clean edges with no pulled paint.

TRANSPARENT PAINTING ON INSIDE OF JARS

Use transparent glass paint or a gloss enamel acrylic paint thinned with a clear medium recommended for that paint. When mixing glass paint and medium, mix so the paint flows freely and is transparent when dry. Test on a spare, recycled jar to test proportions.

1. Pour approximately ½ to 1 ounce of paint into the jar. Turn and let the paint coat the entire inside surface.

2. Pour out the excess paint into a small container or another jar.

3. Set the jar upside down into a plastic container to let the excess paint drip from the jar.

4. When it has stopped dripping, remove from the container and wipe the top clean. Let it completely dry standing right side up. Repeat if you prefer a deeper color.

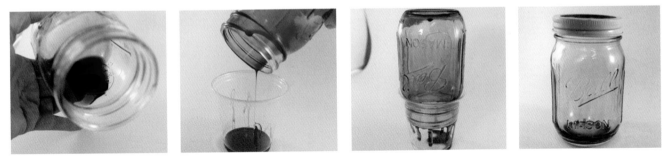

WORKING TIPS

- To hold the jar while decorating and painting, place your hand inside the jar to keep fingerprints off the outside and the paint from smudging.
- Fold an old towel and place it on the work surface to create a "cradle" to hold the jar steady.
- Place a clean sheet of white paper in clear glass jars while decorating so you can see your work in progress.
- Allow enough time. Decorate the jar and allow the paint and glue to cure fully before adding the contents.
- Provide instructions for care when giving a gift. If your finished decorated jar needs any special care, write down the instructions and give them to the recipient with the gift.

STENCILING

You can stencil designs using a precut, purchased stencil or a design you cut yourself from freezer paper.

CUTTING YOUR OWN STENCILS

1. Photocopy the pattern. Tape the copy on a piece of freezer paper that is shiny side up and 1″ larger all around than the pattern.
2. Place the papers on a cutting mat and cut out the motifs with a sharp craft knife.

3. It's very easy to cut out several layers of freezer paper, so for a repeated motif, simply fold a strip of freezer paper and cut the motif only once.
4. You can also use a die and die-cutting machine to cut multiple stencils very easily.

Hand-cut freezer paper stencils.

Die-cut stencils

STENCILING TECHNIQUE:

1. Spray the backside of the stencil with a coat of spray adhesive. (This makes your stencil adhere to the jar and allows you to remove it without tearing.) Let the adhesive dry for 10 minutes and position the stencil on the jar. Or, use masking tape to attach the stencil to the jar.
2. Place a puddle of paint onto a palette or a disposable plate. Load a makeup sponge or stencil brush with paint by dabbing it into the puddle of paint.
3. Press or dab on paper towels to remove excess paint from the applicator. The key here is to use very little paint. Glass is not forgiving; even a little too much paint can seep under the stencil, so it's better to use very little paint and apply as many coats as necessary to achieve the effect you want.
4. Stipple the color into the open areas of the stencil with an up and down dabbing motion. Note: The circular, swirling method of stenciling does not work on the slick glass surface.

USING PAINT PENS

Paint pens are available in many colors and in fine, medium, and calligraphy chisel-point tips. Use them to add accents and lettering to jars or for details and outlines. They can be added to the plain glass surface or to a painted surface. Be sure the basecoat of paint is fully dry and cured before using a paint pen on it. Always test the pens on the bottom of the jar to make sure they are compatible with the glass paint used.

DISTRESSING

Easily distress a jar using a fine sanding block or an emery board. Wait until the paint is fully dried, but before baking in the oven for a complete cure. Lightly sand the paint to remove as much as you like. Embossed jars are especially nice to distress as you can remove paint from the raised area to create a natural worn look.

DOTS

Circular sponges with a flat bottom come in a variety of sizes for adding a quick polka-dot design. Fully load the sponge with paint. Lightly dab sponge into the jar surface, trying not to press too much but enough to apply the paint. The dots will dry with a very textured surface.

OMBRÉ SPONGED TECHNIQUE

This popular effect often used on walls looks beautiful on glass jars!

1. Choose white and another hue for your jar. Mix the white and color with a 50/50 mix or until you have a medium color. Place the white, medium hue, and darker hue in separate areas on a wax paper palette.

2. Use a wedge-type makeup sponge and coat the entire jar with the white paint using an up-and-down pouncing stroke. Be sure to get a good solid coat.

3. While the paint is still wet and using the same sponge applicator, load it with the medium hue. Start in the middle of the jar and work the color around the jar, blending into the white and painting to the bottom of jar. Leave some of the pure white at the top.

4. Load the sponge applicator with the darkest hue. Start at the bottom and paint upward, blending into the medium hue. You want the color to blend nicely from white to the darkest hue with no obvious paint strokes showing.

DIMENSIONAL PAINTING

Dimensional acrylic enamel paint can be used to add raised designs to a jar. You can use the paint to outline areas or make designs. To create an embossed look, after the paint has dried completely, basecoat solidly over the design. Paint over the dried dimensional paint using any of the basecoating techniques. To achieve an even, matte finish with the gloss enamel paints, stipple the paint with a light touch using a large, natural brush while the final paint coat is still wet. This is the technique used for the faux milk glass or a faux hobnail glass look shown here.

PAINTED JARS PROJECTS

Faux Mercury Glass

This is a popular vintage finish for an antique-looking jar.

Using Metallic Silver Spray Paint: Simply spray paint the outside of your jar. Distress it with sanding when dry, if desired.

Using Mirror Spray Paint: This paint is designed to spray into the inside of the jar for a mirrored look that mimics actual mercury glass. It will go on dull and as it dries it will change to a bright reflective finish. To distress this finish, spray a 50/50 mix of water and white vinegar into the jar while the paint is still wet. Gently rub in small circular motions with a paper towel that has also been sprayed with the water/vinegar mixture. This breaks up the paint into interesting cracks and textures. Let dry. Finish with one more light spray.

Red, White, and Blue

Supplies

Pint canning jars

Acrylic enamel paints: cream, red, blue, silver

Clear medium

Star stencil (Use a purchased stencil or cut one from freezer paper.)

Stars cut from freezer paper

Star stickers

1" basecoating brush

1/2" flat artist brush

Foam wedge applicator

Masking tape, 1/2" and 1/4"

Repositionable adhesive spray

Metal lid rings

Spray paint: white

HORIZONTAL RED-STRIPED VASE

1. Basecoat the outside of jar with cream acrylic enamel paint. Be sure to get a solid coverage using several coats of paint.

2. Using a 1/2" flat brush, load the brush fully into the red acrylic paint. Move the brush in one motion around the jar to paint the red stripes. Also paint the neck of the jar. Let paint dry.

STARS VOTIVE HOLDER

1. Mix the silver acrylic enamel paint with a clear medium to a pourable consistency. Basecoat the inside of the jar with this silver paint mixture.

2. Cut out large stars from freezer paper. Apply repositionable adhesive to the back of the stars and place them on jars in a random position.

3. Place the smaller star stickers on the jar among the larger stars.

4. Basecoat the jar solidly with blue acrylic enamel paint using a foam wedge applicator in an up-and-down pouncing technique. Remove the stars when paint has dried.

5. Spray paint the metal lids with white spray paint.

VERTICAL RED-STRIPED VOTIVE HOLDER

1. Mix the silver acrylic enamel paint with a clear medium to a pourable consistency. Basecoat the inside of the jar with this silver paint mixture.

2. Use 1/4" masking tape to tape off the stripes. Paint the jar with a red acrylic enamel paint with as many coats as needed to achieve an opaque coverage. Remove tape when paint has dried.

3. Spray paint the metal lid with white spray paint.

OPAQUE STARS JAR

1. Basecoat the jar with cream acrylic enamel paint.

2. Cut a star stencil from freezer paper and attach to the jar with masking tape.

3. Stencil the stars onto the jar with blue acrylic enamel paint using a foam wedge applicator. Let the first row of stars dry completely before adding additional rows.

Whimsical Blossoms

Supplies

Pint canning jars, vintage green*

Acrylic enamel paints: yellow, white, blue, and green

1" basecoat brush

Masking tape

#4 round artist paint brush

Metal lid rings

Note: my jars were green, but a clear jar is just as pretty.

BLUE-BAND JAR

1. Using masking tape, mask off a 2"-wide band around the middle of the jar. Using blue acrylic enamel paint and the basecoat brush, paint inside the masked off area to create a band with straight edges. Let dry completely, and then remove the tape.

2. Paint white dots for the flower centers at the painted edge of the band by dipping the handle end of a paintbrush in a puddle of paint and dotting on. Paint the dots approximately $3/4"$–1" apart. Some of the dots can be slightly above and below the blue edge.

3. With a #4 round brush loaded into yellow paint, add five flower petals per flower. Clean the brush.

4. Load the #4 brush with green paint to add random green leaves with a dabbing motion.

YELLOW-BAND JAR

1. Using masking tape, mask off a 2" wide band around the middle of the jar. With yellow acrylic enamel paint and the basecoat brush, paint inside the masked off area to create a band with straight edges. Let dry completely, and then remove the tape.

2. Paint white dots for the flower centers at the painted edge of the yellow band by dipping the handle end of a paintbrush in a puddle of paint and dotting on. Paint the dots approximately $3/4"$–1" apart. Some of the dots can be slightly above and below the band edge.

3. With a #4 round brush loaded into blue paint, add five blue flower petals per flower. Clean the brush.

4. Load the #4 brush with green paint to add random green leaves with a dabbing motion.

CLEAR-BAND JAR

1. Using masking tape, mask off a 1" wide band around the bottom of the jar, and a 1" band around the top of the jar. With yellow acrylic enamel paint and the basecoat brush, paint inside the masked off areas to create bands with straight edges. Let dry completely, and then remove the tape.

2. Paint white dots for the flower centers at the bottom painted edge of the top band and the top edge of the bottom band by dipping the handle end of a paintbrush in a puddle of paint and dotting on. Paint the dots approximately $3/4"$ - 1" apart. Some of the dots can be slightly above and below the yellow edge.

3. With a #4 round brush loaded into blue paint, add five blue flower petals per flower. Clean the brush.

4. Load the #4 brush with green paint to add random green leaves with a dabbing motion.

Add white dots for flower centers.

Add petals.

Add leaves.

Etched-Glass Apothecary Jars

These elegant accents for a bathroom or dressing table keep cotton balls, cotton swabs, and make-up sponges right at your fingertips. The glass jars were painted with the faux etched-glass technique while the lids and glass candlesticks were painted using the faux mercury-glass technique.

Supplies

Apothecary type jars with straight sides and lids

Glass candlestick holders for jar stands

1/4" masking tape

Stencil in an all-over pattern

Acrylic enamel paint: white

Clear acrylic enamel medium

Stencil brush

Metallic spray paint: silver

Emery board

JAR DECORATION

1. Use 1/4" masking tape to attach the stencil to the outside of the jar.

2. Make a 50/50 mix of white acrylic glass paint and clear-glass acrylic medium. TIP: Test the mix on the bottom of the jar—you want a translucent white effect.

3. Load the stencil brush with the paint mixture and dab on the paint. Don't overload the stencil brush or the paint may bleed underneath the stencil.

4. Remove the tape and stencil while the paint is fresh. Set the jar aside to dry.

LID AND STAND DECORATION

1. For the lids and candlestick stands, spray with several coats of metallic-silver paint.

2. When dry, distress the paint using an emery board.

Chalkboard-Label Jars

Perfect for storage containers in the kitchen, these jars have chalkboard labels and lids for labeling what's inside.

Supplies

Quart canning jars—plain with no embossing

Label stencil—purchased stencil or make one yourself using freezer paper and a label die

Masking tape

Chalkboard acrylic enamel paint

Foam wedge applicator

White paint pen or chalk pencil

Flat metal lid and screw-on band

Jute

Multi glue

JAR DECORATION

1. Tape the stencil to the front of the jar using masking tape.
2. Using chalkboard acrylic enamel paint, stencil on the label using a wedge-type sponge applicator. The up-and-down pouncing will produce a matte surface that will take chalked lettering well.
3. Remove the stencil and let dry.
4. Use a white paint pen to add a white outline to the black label.
5. Add the lettering using a white paint pen for permanent lettering, or a chalk pencil for erasable lettering.

LID DECORATION

1. Basecoat the metal lids with the chalkboard acrylic paint using the foam-wedge applicators.
2. Add the lettering using a white paint pen for permanent lettering, or a chalk pencil for erasable lettering.
3. Cover the sides of the metal bands with the multi glue and let dry until clear and sticky.
4. Wrap the jute around the sides of the bands to cover.

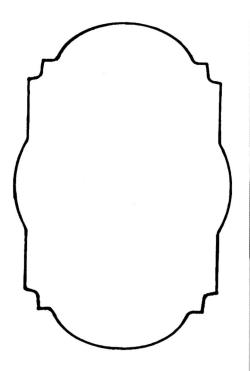

Stencils attached to jars ready for adding paint.

Faux-Antique Milk Glass

These jars mimic the look of vintage milk glass. The jars can be used as containers or simply as beautiful accents.

Supplies

Small wire bail jars, choose jars with straight sides

White dimensional outline acrylic enamel paint

White acrylic enamel paint

Pattern traced onto tracing paper

Paper towels

Basecoating brush

JAR DECORATION

1. Trace the patterns and place them inside the jars. Hold in place with a little masking tape and paper towels in the jar.

2. Outline the designs with white dimensional paint. TIP: Be careful not to apply too much paint; if you do, the design could sag or drip. Lay the jars on your work surface with the painted sides up. Let dry completely.

3. Basecoat the outside of the jar with white paint.

Paisley-Label Jar

Quickly add a paisley label design to a jar using paint pens! This repurposed jar could hold tea or spiced-drink mixes for a great gift idea. Look for the recipes in the Culinary Gifts section.

Supplies

Recycled jar

Paint pens: gold and black

Pattern traced onto tracing paper

Paper towels

Acrylic enamel paint: black

Basecoating brush

JAR DECORATION

1. Trace the patterns and place them inside the jar. Hold in place with a little masking tape and paper towels in the jar.

2. Fill in the paisley shapes with the gold paint pen. Let dry.

3. Add the details using the black paint pen.

LID DECORATION

Basecoat the lid using the black acrylic enamel paint.

Distressed Twine Jar

This is a handy gift to give a home cook or a crafty friend. A ball of twine is an essential supply that has many uses in the kitchen and in the studio. Placing it in this practical jar not only keeps the twine clean, but it dispenses without knots in the twine and allows for easy unwinding and use.

Supplies

Canning jar with decorative embossing on glass and metal seal with screw-on band

Acrylic enamel paint: cream

Basecoating brush

Sandpaper block or emery board

Drill with bit to fit grommet size

Grommets with washers (size to accommodate twine)

Grommet setting tool

Hammer

JAR DECORATION

1. Basecoat the jar with the cream paint.
2. Let the paint dry completely. Distress jar with the sandpaper block or emery board.
3. Using the drill bit, drill a hole in the flat seal lid. The hole should be slightly larger than the center hole of the grommet, and the grommet should fit in snugly. Make this hole in the center of the lid.
4. Follow the manufacturer's directions to set the grommet and washer into the lid.
5. Reassemble the seal and band. Place the twine inside and thread the end through the hole. Screw the lid onto jar.

Distressed Container Jars

Supplies

Small, heavy embossed decorative jars

Acrylic enamel paints: green and light turquoise

Basecoating brush

Sandpaper block or emery board

Hemp twine

JAR DECORATION

1. Basecoat the inside of each jar with a different green paint. Let dry.

2. Basecoat the outside of each jar with the light-turquoise paint.

3. Let the paint dry completely before distressing with the sandpaper block or emery board. Where the outside paint is distressed, the inside color will show through.

4. Wrap the neck of the jar with twine.

Beach Glass Lanterns

These jar lights are perfect for hanging outdoors to illuminate a summer's eve. The colored etched glass appearance is translucent and gives the lights a beautiful glow. The metal collars are easy to create and add a wonderful touch to these lanterns as well as a practical way to hang them.

Supplies

3 mini canning jars

Transparent glass paints: emerald green, dark green, and teal

Wedge sponge applicator

Embossed metal ribbon—one strip per jar

22 gauge wire, 36" piece per jar

Needle-nose pliers

Small clamps

Thin floral wire

JAR DECORATION

Basecoat the jars, each a different color, using the sponge applicator and an up-and-down pouncing motion. This gives the jars a translucent, frosted appearance. You may want to give them more than one coat, depending on how translucent you want them to be. Let dry between each coat.

METAL COLLAR

1. Cut the metal ribbon to fit around the top of the jar plus ½" allowance.

2. Wrap the band around the top of the jar and clamp securely in place.

3. Fold one end of the metal ribbon UP at a 90-degree angle, and the other end DOWN at a 90-degree angle. Hook the angled ends together, and with the pliers, grasp them together and fold down to hold. Use the pliers to squeeze the seam down flat. Remove the metal band from the jar.

4. Fold the 36" wire in half. Twist the wire together to create an 18" piece. Twist the top to form the loop for hanging. Curl both ends using the pliers. At this point you can decide how long you want your hanger to be. If hanging your lights in trees with candles, make sure the wire hanger is long enough to prevent scorching or setting fire to the tree. Secure the wire hanger to the jar with a thin wire.

5. Slip the metal band over the wire loop and onto the neck of the jar.

Citrus Trio

Supplies

Three quart canning jars with screw-on bands

Acrylic enamel paints for glass: white, orange, lime green, yellow, and medium green

Acrylic paints for metal: orange, lime green, and yellow

Black paint pen

Rubber band

Tracing paper and pencil

Transfer paper and stylus

Artist's paint brushes: 1" flat, #4 flat, #3 round, ½" flat

JAR DECORATION

1. Basecoat the outsides of the jars with white acrylic enamel, using a 1" brush. Let dry completely.

2. Trace the patterns (see page 38) onto tracing paper.

3. Transfer the motifs to the jars with transfer paper, using a stylus.

4. Paint the fruits and leaves with acrylic enamels, using a #4 flat brush. TIP: Don't worry about blending the colors or softening your brush strokes—you want a whimsical look. Let dry completely.

5. Add details and outlines to the fruits with the black paint pen.

6. Create the wording upper border by writing the name of the fruit around the top of the jar using a black paint pen. TIP: Keep the border straight by placing a rubber band around the jar where you want the border to be, using the rubber band as a painting guide. When completely dry, remove the rubber band to reveal a perfectly straight border.

7. Follow manufacturers' instructions for curing and care.

LID DECORATION

Paint the bands with acrylic metal paints and a ½" flat brush, using a different color for each lid.

Medium green

Lime green

Yellow

After transferring the pattern, the elements of the design are painted.

The leaf border can be added below the painted design. Outlines and details are added with a black paint pen.

Citrus Trio Patterns

Lemon

Lime

Orange

Good-Dog Goodie Jar

This personalized goodie jar is filled with homemade doggy treats for a best friend! Using paint pens to create a design on a jar is a quick and easy way to personalize it. Choose a font on your computer and design your lettering pattern. See the "Culinary Gifts" chapter for a recipe to make the doggie treats.

Supplies

Large canister jar with lid
White paint pen
Label tag
Red paint pen
Dog charm

JAR DECORATION

1. Create lettering on a computer and print it out. Place the pattern inside the jar and hold in place with masking tape and paper towels stuffed in the jar.
2. Trace and fill in the lettering with the white paint pen. Add paint dots to embellish the lettering.
3. Add the paw prints using the pattern given and white paint pen.
4. Tie a bandana around the neck of the jar for added color.

TAG

Decorate the tag with a dog charm colored with a red paint pen. Add lettering with the white paint pen.

Découpage and Trimmed Jars | PRODUCTS, TECHNIQUES, AND PROJECTS

Découpage is the art of cutting out designs from paper and gluing them to a surface. After the paper designs are glued to the surface, the entire surface is coated with a specially-formulated coating called a decoupage finish or decoupage medium. Most decoupage finishes are multipurpose and can be used to glue the papers to the glass as well as provide the finish coating. Many types of papers can be used to decorate glass jars including wrapping paper, printed napkins, handmade papers, postage stamps, magazine and book pages, and many more.

Jars can also be trimmed and decorated with ribbons, cords, laces, fabrics, and a wide range of materials by simply gluing them onto the jar with glues that are formulated for glass. Glues allow for so much versatility in decorating the jars. This chapter will help you to choose the type of glue you will need for a variety of applications. Choosing the correct glue for a project is important for the success of the finished item.

Jars that are decoupaged or have glued trims cannot be washed and are not meant for food storage. Use these for decorative purposes only. A dry cloth can be used to wipe a surface coated with decoupage finish.

Pictured at right is a close up of a jar from the "Of Eastern Influence" project. Instructions for this jar can be found in this chapter. A page from a Japanese book was decoupaged to a recycled jar.

DÉCOUPAGE & GLUE PRODUCTS

DECOUPAGE MEDIUM

A multi-purpose decoupage medium that can be used for both gluing and sealing paper onto jars is preferable. It dries clear and hard. It can be applied with a brush or sponge applicator. It is water-based so brushes can be cleaned with soap and water after use. Spills can be cleaned up while wet with a damp cloth. Jars with decoupage can be cleaned by wiping with a dry cloth.

ADHESIVE TAPE RUNNERS

There are a variety of adhesive tape runners available in different bonding strengths. Choose a high-performance adhesive runner or one with a strong hold that can be used for adhering heavy embellishments to jars and labels. The removable types of tapes are good for attaching cut-out shapes and stencils to jars. Regular tape runners designed for paper are excellent when creating your recipes and labels. Find these where craft supplies are sold.

SILICONE-BASED ADHESIVE FOR GLASS AND METAL

This type of glue is a very strong adhesive for gluing embellishments to metal and glass. There are a variety of brands on the market. It also works well for gluing fabric to glass, cork to metal, and as a waterproof seal for water-globe jars.

MULTI GLUE

This glue is wonderful for attaching trims, ribbons, and even metallic leaf to jars. It goes on white, and when dry is clear and very sticky, allowing a mess-free application. To use, apply the adhesive with the narrow top applicator for small areas or with the bottom wide applicator for large areas. Let dry completely until clear and sticky. It can be applied to the item you are gluing, or it can be applied to the jar, such as a jar neck. After the glue dries on the neck of the jar, the trim can be applied directly to the sticky adhesive.

GLUE GUN

This is another waterproof glue that is easy to use. It is great for creating a waterproof seal when making water-globe jars. It also works as a quick, strong adhesive when covering jar lids with a padded cover, embellishing jars, or gluing scenes in jars.

REPOSITIONABLE SPRAY ADHESIVE

This glue is great for creating a temporary hold for stencils. Simply give a light spray to the back of the stencil, position the stencil on the glass, and when finished remove stencil.

ADHESIVE TABS

These are small squares or other shapes of adhesive on a peel away paper that you remove and place on your objects to be glued. Be sure to choose a "power" strength tab for gluing items to jars.

PAPER

Many types of papers can be used to decorate jars with the decoupage technique. You can choose to add just a few cut-out motifs or you can cover a jar completely. Lightweight decoupage paper and gift-wrapping paper are the best types of paper for decoupage. Printed napkins, handmade papers, and collage papers are also options.

OTHER SUPPLIES NEEDED

- Sponge brush for applying medium
- Craft knife and sharp scissors "for cutting designs
- Cutting mat to use with a craft knife
- Metal ruler to use for measuring and as a straight edge for cutting
- Freezer paper to cover and protect work surface

HOW TO DÉCOUPAGE

Paper panel with straight edges

GLUING PAPER MOTIFS

Protect your work surface with freezer paper. Using a foam brush, lightly coat the back of the paper with decoupage medium. Position the image on the surface and smooth it with your fingers, pushing out wrinkles and air bubbles. Allow to dry.

GLUING HANDMADE PAPERS, NAPKINS, OR TISSUE

For these delicate papers, apply the decoupage medium to the jar and carefully place on the paper. Use a light touch when positioning and sealing to prevent ripping the paper.

GENERAL SEALING

Apply two to three coats of the decoupage medium with the foam brush to seal the paper. The finish appears cloudy when wet but will dry crystal clear.

CUTTING OUT MOTIFS

Trim away excess paper from around the image you wish to cut out. Use a craft knife and cutting mat to cut out any areas inside the image before cutting around the outer edges. Use small, sharp, pointed scissors to cut around the edge of the design. Hold scissors at a 45-degree angle so the paper is cut with a slightly beveled edge. (The beveled edge helps the image adhere snugly against the surface.)

CUTTING STRAIGHT EDGES

Use a metal ruler, a cutting mat, and a craft knife to cut out panels. Place the ruler, hold down firmly with your non-dominating hand, and using the craft knife, cut a straight edge.

TORN EDGES

Tearing the paper can create an interesting, deckled edge. Tearing the paper toward you and away from you will create different effects. Experiment with a scrap piece of paper to see which you like best for your project.

Decoupaged paper napkins

DÉCOUPAGED AND TRIMMED JARS

Tea & Coffee Canisters

Making specialized canisters is a beautiful way to brighten up and organize a pantry. Canisters also make proud vessels for homemade drink mixes to give as gifts. Decorative card stock has been découpaged in two layers on these jars. The labels were computer generated and printed right onto the card stock. When giving these canisters as a gift, fill them with homemade drink mixes such as "Favorite Tea Blend" or "Spiced-Mocha Coffee Mix." See the "Culinary Gifts" chapter for recipes. Decoupaged projects can be cleaned with a dry or slightly damp cloth but cannot be immersed in water.

Supplies

Quart old-fashioned canning jars with glass lids and wire bails

Card stock in the color of your choice (We used a plain color for the labels and a subtle script pattern for the panels.)

Pencil

Sanding block

Metal ruler

Cloth tape measure

Decoupage medium

Sponge brush

Freezer paper

Circle template with various sizes of circles

Scissors

Optional: Fabric ribbon or trim

JAR DECORATION

1. Create lettering on a computer using a large font size. Experiment with a 72 pt or 84 pt font size to see which works best for your type and size of jar. Print your lettering on your chosen card stock. If needed, cut the card stock to fit your printer.

2. Use light pencil marks to draw a rectangle label shape around the lettering. To allow for more white edging around the edge of the label, use a sanding block to sand the paper lightly to remove the color around the outside of the rectangle you marked. Erase any pencil marks that may remain. Hand tear the paper into a label shape.

3. Measure the size needed to make the card stock panels fit the jars. The panels will be placed on only the straight sides of the jars and not onto the curved sections at the neck and bottom of the jars. The paper is too heavy to conform to the curved surfaces when glued without adhering properly or looking messy. Measure the height needed, and then measure around the jar to determine the circumference. This will be the length to cut the panel. Unless you have a very long piece of card stock, you may need to cut several pieces to make up the length needed. Use a ruler and light pencil marks to draw the panels onto the card stock. Hand tear the panels.

4. Glue the panels to the jars with decoupage medium. Glue the labels on top of the panels. Let dry. Add a top coat of medium onto the paper surface and slightly over the paper edge to help protect and seal the paper.

LID DECORATION

1. Determine what size circle you need to cover lid top for the size lid you have. Use a circle template and trace a circle onto matching card stock. Cut out the circle.

2. Glue and seal the circle to the top of the lid with decoupage medium. Let dry.

3. Depending upon the type of jar you have, there may be an area to add some ribbon or fabric trim to further ornament the jar lid. If so, cut to size and attach with decoupage medium.

Italian Countryside

These bail-style jars make great containers for herbs, tea, or coffee. These jars are découpaged in layers. The first layer is a script card stock, the second layer is an Italian-themed printed napkin. The tops are finished with the script card stock cut into circles. Because decoupaged jars are not recommended for washing but only wiping with a dry or slightly damp cloth, store non-messy items in them. When using jars as gifts, fill them with your favorite mixes and include a recipe card for the mixes. See the "Culinary Gifts" chapter for recipes.

Supplies

Quart and pint canning jars with glass lids and wire bails

Card stock: printed with script design

Paper napkin: printed with landscape design

Metal ruler

Cloth tape measure

Pencil

Scissors

Craft knife

Cutting mat

Decoupage medium

Sponge brush

Freezer paper

Matching ribbon

Circle template with various sizes of circles

Power tab adhesive or silicone-based glue

Wax seal or coin for embellishment

JAR DECORATION

1. Measure and cut the card stock panels to fit completely around the jar on the straight sides and not onto the curved sections at the neck and bottom of the jar. The paper is too heavy to conform to the curved surface without looking messy. For these panels, measure the height of the jar's straight surface, approximately 1" from the top and bottom. This will be the height to cut the panel. Measure around the jar to determine the circumference. This will be the length to cut the panel. Unless you have a very long piece of card stock, you may need to cut several pieces to make up the length needed. To help make a thinner seam where the panels overlap, hand tear the paper at the edges instead of cutting.

2. Glue and seal the card stock panels to the jar with decoupage medium. Let dry.

3. Separate the layers of napkins. Cut the top layer (with the design printed on it) to fit the entire jar from the neck to the bottom. The paper is thin and will conform to the curved surface of the jar. Because it is thin, it will become translucent when applied with decoupage medium so that the under layer of the script paper will show thru, especially in some of the plainer areas of the napkin.

4. Brush decoupage medium onto the entire surface of the jar. Arrange napkin panels onto jar. Carefully brush over the napkin with a heavy coat of découpage medium. Try not to tear the paper—brush lightly or in a dabbing motion. The napkins will wrinkle slightly—let them as that is part of the look. Let dry.

5. Wrap ribbon around the neck of jar. Secure ends with a power tab (or silicone-based glue). Use another power tab or glue to attach your chosen embellishment.

LID DECORATION

1. Use a circle template and trace circles onto script card stock to fit the jar lid. Cut out the circle.

2. Glue and seal the circle to the top of the lid with decoupage medium. Let dry.

Book Page Window Jar

The heart-shaped windows on these lovely decoupaged jars will allow the recipient of these gift jars to see what is within—so make it pretty. They can be used to give a gift of your favorite tea blend or as tea lights to decorate and illuminate! See page 50 for patterns for cutting out a window in your decoupage paper.

Supplies

Pint canning jars with flat metal seals and screw-on bands

Book pages

Metal ruler

Cloth tape measure

Pencil

Scissors

Decoupage medium

Sponge brush

Freezer paper

Wet wipes or damp paper towel

Jute

Kraft tags

JAR DECORATION

1. Measure jar and cut panels from the book page papers to fit the jar. The book page paper is cut in a panel to cover only the straight sides of jar. To cut the book page panel, measure the height of the jar's straight surface, approximately 1″ from the top and bottom. This will be the height to cut the book page panel. Measure around the jar to determine the circumference. This will be the length to cut the panel. Unless you have a very large book page, you may need to cut several pieces to make up the length needed. To help make a thinner seam where the panels overlap, hand tear the paper at edges instead of cutting.

2. Fold the panel that will be at the front of the jar in half. Trace a 1/2 heart motif onto this folded area and cut out your heart. (Patterns are on page 50.)

3. Lightly coat the back of the book page sections with decoupage medium. Position the panels on the jar and smooth with your fingers, pushing out wrinkles and air bubbles. Immediately use a wet wipe or damp paper towel to remove any decoupage medium from the glass. Allow to dry.

4. Apply additional coats of decoupage medium to seal and protect the paper surface. Repeat the wiping off of any decoupage medium on the glass surface. The surface will not be waterproof and should be used for a decorative accessory.

5. Tie a piece of jute twine to the top of the jar. Place a screw-on band onto the jar for a finished appearance.

TAG

Use the cut-out heart to decorate a tag by gluing on with decoupage medium. If using as a votive holder, do not use the flat sealing lid, just the band.

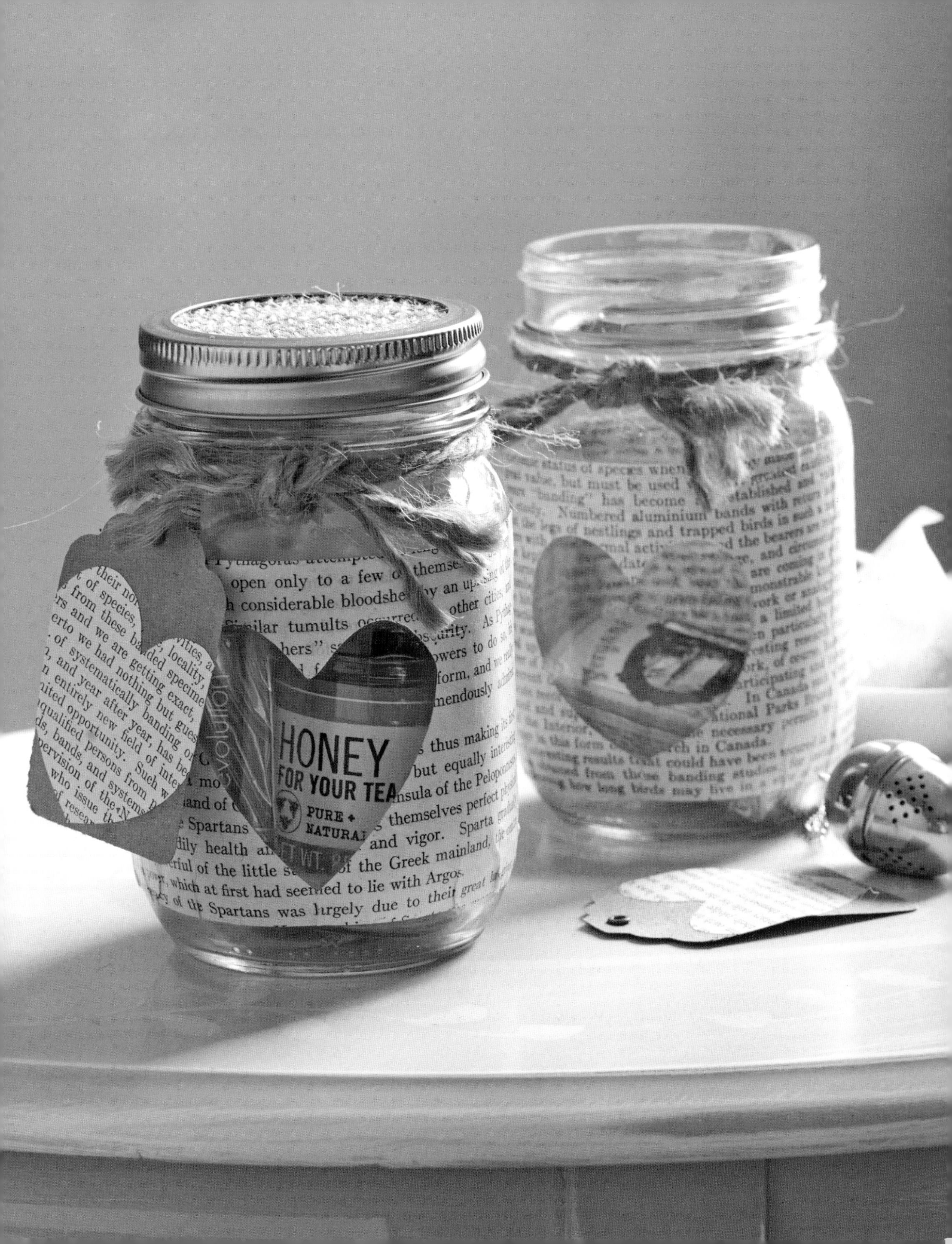
HONEY
FOR YOUR TEA
PURE + NATURAL

Book-Page Window-Jar Patterns

Use any of these shapes to cut a window from you decoupage pages as instructed in the "Book-Page Window Jar" project on page 48.

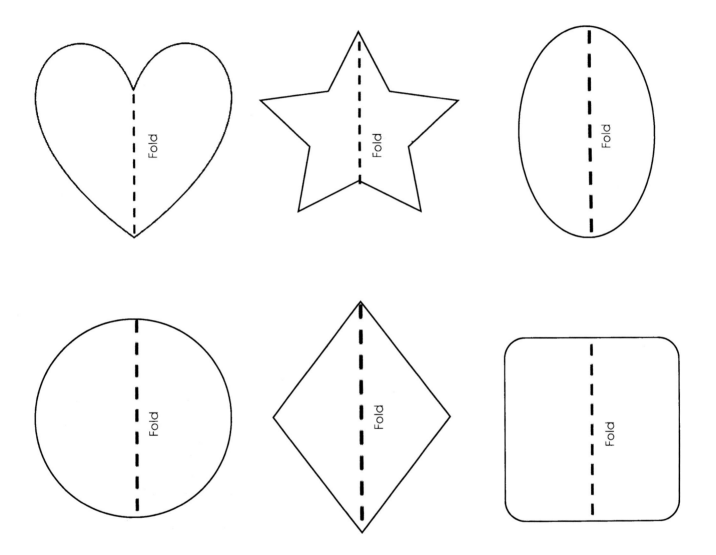

Of Eastern Influence

A set of elegant containers like these would make a lovely gift set for a favorite artist or craftsperson. Fill them with the tools of the trade. A selection of beautiful Japanese rice papers and a book page with Japanese writing are découpaged onto recycled jars to make this attractive set of storage jars.

Supplies

Recycled jars

Selection of green-hued thin Japanese rice papers

Japanese book page

Metal ruler

Cloth tape measure

Pencil

Scissors

Craft knife

Cutting mat

Decoupage medium

Sponge brush

Freezer paper

Raffia or twine in various colors

JAR DECORATION

1. Measure the jars and cut panels from the papers to fit the jars. The rice papers can be cut to cover the entire jar as they are thin enough to conform to the curved surface or can be split and overlapped to fit snugly on surface. The heavier book-page paper is cut in a panel to cover only the straight area of jar. To cut the book-page panel, measure the height of the jar's straight surface, approximately 1" from the top and bottom. This will be the height to cut the book-page panel. Measure around the jar to determine the circumference. This will be the length to cut the panel. Unless you have a very large book page, you may need to cut several pieces to make up the length needed. To help make a thinner seam where the panels overlap, hand tear the paper at edges instead of cutting.

2. Glue the paper panels to the jars with decoupage medium. Because the rice papers are so thin and delicate, it may be easier to apply the glue to the jars in the area where the papers will cover and then place the papers. Smooth the paper with your fingers to minimize wrinkles. Be very careful at this point as the papers are very delicate and can tear easily. Let dry completely.

3. Seal with a top coat of decoupage finish. Let dry.

4. Cover the neck of the jars with a wrapping of raffia and finish with a front knot.

Play Money

This makes a great gift for a child or a friend who is trying to save up for a really great vacation. This jar has a windowed decoupage base—perfect for viewing a money savings as it grows!

Supplies

Small, recycled jar with lid

Play paper money available from novelty shops, 3 bills per jar

Play money coins or foreign coins

Pencil

Craft knife

Cutting mat

Decoupage medium

Sponge brush

Freezer paper

Wet wipes or damp paper towels

Silicone-based glue

JAR DECORATION

1. Fold the bill that will be on the front of the jar in half. Cut out an oval at front center. Some bills have an oval design that can just be cut out.

2. Prepare another bill for the back of jar so that the bills meet at the sides and overlap. To help mask the seams where the papers meet and overlap, tear the ends of papers instead of cutting.

3. Lightly coat the backs of the paper money with decoupage medium. Position the paper on the jar and smooth it with your fingers, pushing out wrinkles and air bubbles. Immediately take the wipe or damp paper towel and remove any decoupage medium from the glass. Allow to dry.

4. Apply additional coats of decoupage medium to seal and protect the paper surface. Repeat the wiping off of any decoupage medium on the glass surface. The surface will not be waterproof and should be used for a decorative accessory rather than for foodstuff.

LID DECORATION

1. Use the third bill to cover the lid. Trim the paper money to roughly fit the lid. Glue the paper down to the top and sides of the lid using decoupage medium. Trim off any excess at bottom edge of lid. Let dry.

2. Seal the paper with two coats of the decoupage medium, allowing to dry between each coat.

3. Arrange and glue coins to the top of the lid using silicone-based glue. Let dry.

Button Collection

Everyone has a button collection, but most people don't have a beautiful jar in which to keep buttons. This pretty jar is a handy receptacle to keep track of all those strays. It will be a welcomed and beautiful gift for a home sewer when filled with vintage buttons or wooden spools. Using buttons all of the same color to glue to the lid makes the lid look like carved ivory.

Supplies

Small, wide-mouth canning jar with flat metal seal and screw-on band (I used an old canning jar with a glass lid, but a newer jar would also work nicely.)

Acrylic metal paint: cream

Sponge applicator

Silicone-based glue

Mother-of-pearl buttons

Pearls

Thick white glue

Decorative trim, 12″ long, cream

Glue gun and glue stick

LID DECORATION

1. Paint the metal ring and flat lid seal with a cream acrylic metal paint. Let dry.
2. Glue the seal into the metal ring with silicone-based glue, being careful not to get glue on screw-on area of lid.
3. Glue the buttons in place with silicone-based glue, being careful with glue so it won't show. Add a few pearls for accents. Let dry.
4. Glue cream trim around the lid using the glue gun.

Beachfront Property

This jar will help recall the fun of a family beach vacation. Fill the jar with shells and other mementos from the trip and give it to your friend or family member who shared your trip. It will bring back treasured memories year after year.

Supplies

Tall, straight sided recycled jar with lid

Coral gravel: white (from an aquarium shop)

Shells

Acrylic enamel paint: cream

Thick white glue ("tacky" type that won't run)

Sponge applicator

Silicone-based glue

Kraft tag

Marker

Twine

JAR

Fill the bottom of the jar with the white coral gravel. Add collected shells or other vacation memorabilia.

LID DECORATION

1. If needed, paint the lid with the cream acrylic enamel paint. Let dry.
2. Cover the lid with a heavy coat of white glue. Sprinkle with the coral gravel to cover. Let dry.
3. Coat the gravel on the lid with a coat of the white glue. Let dry.
4. Adhere an arrangement of shells onto the lid using the silicone-based glue. Be careful to not use too much glue. You want to glue the shells together and to the lid so that glue is not evident. Let dry.

EMBELLISHMENTS

Write a sentiment on the tag. Attach the tag with a piece of twine.

Honey Jar

Who wouldn't like to have a jar of honey as a gift? This is perfect to bring to the hostess of your next dinner party. Cork is used for the decorative letters. It is a very versatile and attractive product for decorating jars! Thin sheets of cork or cork ribbon are available both plain and with added adhesive for easy application. Find these where craft supplies are sold.

Supplies

Half-pint canning jar with flat metal seal and screw-on band

Thin cork sheeting

Cork ribbon

Repositionable spray adhesive

Craft knife

Cutting mat

Metal Ruler

Silicone-based adhesive

Bee charm

Pencil

Rubber stamp, bee design or motif of your choice

Permanent ink pad: black

Optional: Alphabet die and die cutting machine

JAR DECORATION

1. If you are using an alphabet die with a die cutting machine, cut out the word "HONEY" from the cork sheeting. or print out the word "HONEY" from a font on your computer. Experiment with an 84 pt. or 96 pt. narrow font to see which works best for your size jar. Use this as a pattern to cut out cork letters from cork sheeting. To do this, spray the backside of the paper pattern with spray adhesive. Place the cork piece on a cutting mat and then place the lettering pattern over the cork. Use a craft knife to cut out letters. Peel pattern away when cutting is complete.

2. Apply silicone glue to the back of lettering and place on the front of the jar. If you are using cork with adhesive backing, simply remove the backing and place lettering on jar. For best spacing, adhere the middle letter "N" first and then other letters.

3. Glue a bee charm to the jar for added accent.

LID DECORATION

1. Cut the cork ribbon to the width of the screw-on band. Apply glue to the ribbon (or remove the adhesive backing from cork) and position on the rim of the band. Alternatively, you can cut strips of cork from a cork sheet to size using a craft knife and cutting mat.

2. Use the flat metal seal as a pattern to trace a circle onto the cork sheet. Cut this out with a craft knife.

3. Stamp your chosen motif into the center of cork circle using the black inkpad. Remove the adhesive backing or use a silicone-based glue to attach cork circle to the metal seal.

Gilded Label Jar

This golden treasure jar, decorated with metal leafing, would be a great receptacle for a variety of items to give as gifts or a beautiful gift on its own. It is not recommended for food products as metal leaf can not be washed. Metal leafing can be adhered to glass with liquid leaf adhesive, spray adhesive, double-sided tape, or a multi glue that dries clear and sticky. It is available at craft or art supply stores. It can also be used on metal lids and gift tags.

Supplies

Pint canning jar with flat metal seal and screw-on band

Variegated metal leaf

Multi glue

Soft brush

Freezer paper

Card stock: black

Oval template with 2½" wide oval

Pencil

Scissors

Gold paint pen

Spray paint: black

JAR DECORATION

1. Brush a thin coat of multi glue onto the surface you wish to leaf. Let dry until clear and sticky.

2. Carefully place a leaf sheet on the tacky surface. Using the soft brush, gently brush leaf to smooth it onto adhesive. Pounce it gently to get it into any crevices. Keep placing leaf until entire jar is covered. Use a clean dry brush to swish away excess flakes of leaf.

3. Use an oval template to trace an oval onto the black card stock. Cut out oval template. Add lettering and dotted border to the oval using the gold paint pen.

4. Brush multi glue onto the back of the oval label. Allow glue to dry until clear and sticky. Attach the black oval label to the jar.

LID DECORATION

Basecoat the metal seal and screw-on band with the black spray paint.

Quick Tricks | PROJECTS AND INSTRUCTIONS

There are a multitude of ways you can decorate jars quickly and easily while having lots of fun making great gifts for family and friends. In the following chapter are some beautifully creative tricks for decking out your jars so that they are not only pretty, but also they are useful. With simple trims and embellishments, your jars can go from ordinary to extraordinary.

By doing a neat trick with the lids, you will see ways to turn jars into drinking mugs, liquid soap dispensers, and yarn caddies. With a little fabric, trim, and poly fiberfil you can make clever and useful pincushions and sewing kit jars. Turn jar lids upside down, place an insert using the ideas shown to turn the lids into coasters. Snow globes, terrarium-like scenery jars, and jars decorated with fabric, ribbons, and trims are some of the interesting tricks you will learn for making plain jars into special gifts.

A gift is not complete without a label or a tag. This chapter will give tips for finding the supplies needed as well as useful techniques for making personalized labeling.

Pictured left is a tag that adorns a jar of bird seed to give to a bird-watcher friend. Tags not only label the contents to give needed information, but they also dress up the jar. Instructions follow in this chapter for creating the "Picnic for the Birds" jar. Pictured right are "Fruit Sewing Kits." See page 62 for instructions.

Fruit Sewing Kits

These fruit-themed jars have pincushion tops and mini sewing kits inside. They're a perfect bazaar item or office gift. Instead of polyester batting, the pincushion is created with a plastic foam ball.

Basic Supplies

Small jars with lids (Recycled baby food jars would work well for this project.)

2″ plastic foam ball, 1 per jar

Serrated knife

Felt

Scissors

Cloth tape measure

Glue gun and clear glue stick

Fabric rickrack trim

Silk pink blossoms

Sewing kit contents: needles, safety pins, and thimbles

BASIC LID DECORATION

1. Cut away one-third of the plastic foam ball using a serrated knife to create a flat bottom.

2. Cut a 6″ circle of felt. Cut leaves from green felt, cutting as many as you would like to use for decoration. See pictured jars for inspiration. Cut a ½″-wide band of green felt in a length needed to fit around the rim of the lid.

3. Place the felt circle, centered over the round top of the foam ball. Stretch the fabric around the ball and glue the excess fabric onto the flat bottom with a glue gun.

4. Glue the ball on the top of the lid, using the glue gun and a large amount of glue. Hold firmly in place until cool and secure.

5. Use light dots of hot glue to attach the trims to the lid. Glue the ½″ band of felt around the rim of the lid. Glue the green leaves in place. Add a piece of color coordinated rickrack around the rim of the lid, covering bottom edges of leaves. Add silk blossoms to cover the seam and add a decorative finish.

6. Fill the jar with sewing notions of your choice. A 2″ x 5″ strip of felt cut with pinking shears holds a few needles and some safety pins.

7. Add a few decorative pins to the pincushion.

PEACH JAR SUPPLIES AND INSTRUCTIONS

Felt cut into a 6″ circle: yellow

Silk blossoms: pink

Felt for leaves and band: green

Fabric rickrack trim: green

Blush makeup: pink

1. After cutting away a third of the ball to make a flat bottom, create an indent by placing ball on the edge of a counter and pressing.

2. Cover the ball with felt as instructed. Using a needle and strong thread, reinforce this indent by making one large stitch from the top to the bottom of the ball. Secure the thread. Add a little blush to the peach for added color.

STRAWBERRY JAR SUPPLIES AND INSTRUCTIONS

Felt cut into a 6" circle: red

Silk blossoms: pink

Felt for leaves and band: green

Fabric rickrack trim: red

Headed pins: white

1. Follow the previous instructions for making the pincushion lid. For this jar, the green felt leaves were cut with pinking shears.
2. Glue the white headed pins into the pincushion.

BLUEBERRY JAR SUPPLIES AND INSTRUCTIONS

Felt cut into a 6" circle: blue

Silk blossoms: pink

Felt for leaves and band: green

Fabric rickrack trim: blue

Headed pin: blue

1. Follow the previous instructions for making the pincushion lid.
2. Glue the blue-headed pin into the center top of the pincushion.

Globe Jar Top

All kinds of miniature items can be used to compose three dimensional arrangements on jar lids that will turn a simple jar into a special hostess gift. Use the arrangements to extend a theme, like the shells for a beach theme, or as an embellishment for a jar of jam or honey. This festive winter-themed jar top is perfect to fill with a hot chocolate mix! See the "Culinary Gifts" chapter for recipe.

Supplies

Recycled jar with white lid

Plastic globe, 2-part type used for Christmas ornaments (1/2 per top)

Arrangement elements: miniature bottlebrush trees and plastic deer

Crystal beads: 10mm

Craft glue: white

Glitter

Decorative fabric trim or ribbon

Scissors

Glue gun with clear glue sticks

LID DECORATION

1. Arrange the trees, deer, and beads onto the top of the jar lid. Occasionally place the clear globe to check the fit of the elements inside the globe.

2. Add an additional layer of glue to the base and the trees and sprinkle with glitter while glue is still wet. Let dry and brush off any excess glitter. Make sure the glue has dried completely before continuing with the next step.

3. Using the white glue, adhere the 1/2 clear globe on the top of the lid, closing in the arrangement.

4. Determine the amount of trim needed to surround the bottom seam of the globe. Cut to fit. With the glue gun, attach the trim around the base of the globe.

Coiled-Rope Coasters

These coasters are the perfect gift for someone with a seaside cottage or beach-themed home. They are easy and fun to make and will delight any hostess. To keep the coiled rope from staining, spray it with a fabric protector.

Supplies

Large, wide mouth screw-on bands

Soft rope, ¼" diameter

Cork sheet

Mat board: cream

Pencil

Craft knife

Cutting mat

Scissors

Multi glue

Freezer paper

Fabric protective spray

LID DECORATION

1. Use a screw-on band as a template to trace circles onto the mat board, one per coaster. Cut out circles using the craft knife. Check to make sure these circles will fit into your lid bands. Adjust if necessary.

2. Use a screw-on band as a template to trace circles onto a cork sheet, one per coaster. Cut out circles from cork sheet.

3. Place the screw-on bands on your surface, with the inside of the bands facing up. Glue the mat board circles, right side up, into the bands using the multi glue. Weight the mat board down with an empty jar until the glue is dry.

4. Cover the mat board on the inside of the bands with a heavy coat of multi glue and let dry until clear and sticky. Start in the center of the lid and coil the rope into the lid. Trim off the excess and tuck the cut end into the edge with the tip of a pair of scissors.

5. Coat the bottom of the coasters (which is the top of the screw-on bands) with multi glue and let dry until clear and sticky. Glue the cork circles onto the bottoms of the coasters.

6. Spray the rope surface with a fabric protector.

Stamped Cork Jar-Lid Coasters

These practical coasters are lined with cork that soaks up condensation from cold drinks. Decorate the surface with a rubber stamp design that is personalized to your gift recipient.

Supplies

Quart-size flat metal seal and screw-on band

Thin cork sheeting

Pencil

Scissors

Rubber stamp: grapes

Permanent ink pad: black

Multi glue (if your cork sheeting is not self-adhesive)

Silicone-based adhesive

LID DECORATION

1. Use the flat metal seal as a pattern to trace a circle onto the cork sheet. Cut out the circle. Stamp your chosen motif onto the center of the cork circle using the black inkpad. Remove the adhesive backing from cork or apply multi glue to the back of the cork circle and allow to dry until tacky. Attach the cork to the inside of the metal seal.

2. Glue the cork-covered metal seal to the inside of the screw-on band, right side up, using silicone-based glue. Weight down the seal using an empty jar until dry.

Cozy Jar Collection

These jars are covered with a canvas wrap that comes off easily so that jars can be washed. We filled our jars with comfort food mixes for much appreciated gifts. See the "Culinary Gifts" chapter for recipes for soup or bread mixes. Be sure to include the recipe cards for cooking the mixes into a delicious meal. We attached decorative cotton tags to our jars, but you may wish to make your own tags of paper or cloth with the gift recipient's name or to list the contents of the jar.

Supplies

Quart and pint canning jars with both wide and narrow openings

Flat metal seals and screw-on bands

Canvas fabric, 1/4 yd.

Ruler

Measuring tape

Scissors

Sewing needle

Thread to match fabric

Pencil

Hook-and-loop tabs, self-adhesive

Cotton tags (or make your own paper or fabric tags)

Buttons

Butcher twine: black and white

Measuring tape fabric ribbon

Mini clothespins

JAR DECORATION

1. Measure the height and the circumference of the jar to determine the size to cut the fabric panel. Add 3" to the circumference measurement to determine the length to cut the fabric panel. Cut out a fabric panel for each jar. Fray the top and bottom edges of the panels by pulling the warp threads.

2. Fold 1/2" hems on both ends of the canvas panels and iron. Fold again another 1/2" at each end. This will eliminate raw edges on the fabric panel ends. Sew the hems with a line of hand stitching.

3. Wrap the canvas panels around the jars, overlapping the ends. Mark the panels where they overlap in the area to add the hook-and-loop tabs, positioned for a snug fit. Attach hook-and-loop tabs.

4. The wraps were decorated in three different ways as follows:
- A row of sewn-on buttons.
- A wrap of black-and-white butcher twine
- A wrap of cloth measuring tape ribbon with a knot tied in the front.

5. Attach the labels to the jars with the twine.

6. Recipes for the culinary mixes can be attached to the jar coverings with the mini clothespins for added embellishment.

Fabric-Topped Padded Lids

Fabric-topped lids are easy, traditional toppers for food gifts. You may recall your grandmother's jelly jars topped with decorative fabric circles. By padding these fabric lids with fiberfill, they now take on an entirely new look. Use cotton fabrics or cotton-polyester blends for best results. The puffy lids can also be used as pin cushions, with the jars holding sewing supplies. We used metal ribbon to wrap around the band edge, covering the edge of the glued puffy top. Feel free to use a sturdy fabric trim to cover edge if you can't find metal ribbon. When using jars for food gifts, fill them with your favorite mixes and include a recipe card for the mixes. See the "Culinary Gifts" chapter for recipes.

Supplies

Two flat metal seals and one screw-on band per jar

Fabric of your choice

Polyester batting

Pencil

Glue gun with clear glue sticks

Cloth tape measure

Scissors

Sewing needle

Thread to match fabric

Silicone-based adhesive

Metal ribbon, 1" width (found in craft supply stores)

Small clamps

Needle-nosed pliers

LID DECORATION

1. Use a flat seal as a template to cut a piece of batting. Double or triple the batting depending how padded you wish the top to be. Glue the batting to the top of one of the seals with a glue gun.

2. Cut out a fabric circle for each jar lid. Cut a 4.5" diameter for standard jars, 6" diameter for wide-mouth jars.

3. With needle and double thread, sew a running stitch completely around circle, 1/2" in from the edge of the fabric circle. Leave the needle and thread attached. Position the fabric over the batting. Pull the thread to gather the fabric tightly around the under side of the seal. Sew a few stitches to hold the gathering and knot and cut the thread.

4. Using silicone-based adhesive, glue the padded lid to the top of the screw-on band.

5. The jar can be sealed using the remaining flat seal, or you can glue the second seal into the inside of the band to hide the gathered fabric.

6. Cut the metal ribbon to fit around the screw-on band plus 1/2".

7. Wrap the ribbon around the band and clamp it securely in place.

8. Fold one end of the metal ribbon UP at a 90-degree angle, and the other end DOWN at a 90-degree angle. Hook the angled ends together, and with the pliers, grasp them together and fold down to hold. Use the pliers to squeeze the seam down flat to the band. Crimp the collar on tightly so that it will not need to be glued.

1. Cut a fabric circle to cover the lid.
2. Gather the fabric on the bottom side of flat lid seal.
3. Glue the lid seal to the top of the screw-on band.
4. Clamp the metal ribbon to the screw-on band to cover sides.
5. Secure the metal ribbon where the edges meet.

3

4

5

2

1

Pincushion Button Jar

Here is a cute, handy little jar filled with buttons that would make a great hostess or teacher gift! Instead of polyester batting, the pincushion is created with a handful of polyester fiberfill and the seal is glued inside the band instead of on top like was done for Fruit Sewing Kits.

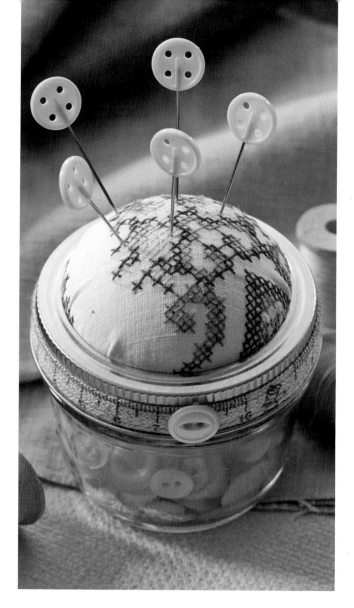

Supplies

Small canning jar with flat metal seal and screw-on band

Vintage linen or embroidery piece

Pencil

Scissors

Sewing needle

Thread matching fabric

Polyester fiberfill

Glue gun and glue sticks

Fabric glue

Measuring tape fabric ribbon or other decorative ribbon

Buttons

Button-topped pins

LID DECORATION

1. Cut a fabric circle that is 6" in diameter from the vintage fabric piece. Use the metal seal as a template to cut another piece of fabric to the size of the lid.

2. Using the larger fabric piece, sew a running stitch with double thread completely around the circle, 1/2" in from edge. Leave needle and thread attached. Pull the thread slightly to gather, leaving at least a 2½"–3" opening. Stuff with polyester fiberfill. Place this over the flat lid seal and pull thread tightly to gather it on the under side of lid seal piece. Make a few stitches to hold the gathering and knot and cut the thread.

3. Run a bead of hot glue around the top inside of the screw-on band. Quickly, place the metal seal lid inside band, pushing the padded top up above the band and being careful not to get glue on the fabric. Immediately place the lid assembly on the jar and screw tightly to hold while drying.

4. Cover the inside of the lid with the smaller fabric circle using fabric glue. This will conceal the gathered bottom of lid.

5. Glue the measuring tape ribbon around outside of band using the glue gun. Glue a button to conceal the seam and to add an accent.

6. Place some decorative pins in the pincushion before giving it as a gift.

Vintage Lid Pincushions

Simple and fun to make and a great gift for your favorite home sewer, these lid pincushions were created with vintage linens.

Supplies

Flat metal seal and screw-on band

Vintage linen fabric piece

Pencil

Cork sheet

Scissors

Sewing needle

Thread to match fabric

Polyester fiberfill

Glue gun and glue sticks

LID DECORATION

1. Using the flat metal seal as a template, trace a circle onto the cork sheet and cut it out.

2. Cut a fabric circle 6″ in diameter from the linen. Sew a running stitch with double thread completely around the circle, ½″ in from edge. Leave needle and thread attached. Pull the thread slightly to gather, leaving at least a 2½″–3″ opening. Stuff with polyester fiberfill. Place this over the flat lid seal and pull the thread tightly to gather it on the under side of lid seal piece. Make a few stitches to hold the gathering and knot and cut the thread.

3. Place the screw-on band on your work surface, under side up. Run a bead of hot glue around the top inside of the metal band. Quickly place the cork circle into the band, right side down. Allow to dry.

4. Apply some glue to side of the cork piece that is facing up, and position the pincushion into the lid on top of the glued-down cork.

Spa in a Jar

This jar is packed with everything needed for a relaxing "spa day" and decorated with "diamonds"—a girl's best friend! You can also use recycled jars and lids for this project.

Supplies

Wide mouth quart canning jar with flat metal seal and screw-on band

Lacey fabric

Glue gun and glue sticks

Scissors

Decorative ribbons: several types such as gathered tulle ribbon and narrow velvet ribbon

Ribbon rosette

Vintage rhinestone brooch

Rhinestone charm with split ring

Rhinestone trim with adhesive backing

Decorative individual rhinestones or other shiny gems

Glass vials with cork stoppers, small enough to fit into the quart jar

Small gift soaps and other items to fill the jar

Rice paper or handmade papers

JAR DECORATION

1. Glue the metal seal into the screw-on band using hot glue. Allow this to dry.

2. Cover the top of the lid with a lace fabric circle, bringing it down over the edge of the band. Allow glue to dry and then trim the edges of the fabric even with the edge of band. Cover the rim of the band with the several layers of decorative ribbons using the glue gun and hot glue to attach each. Cover the top of the lid with the ribbon rosette. Glue or pin on the vintage brooch in the middle of the rosette.

3. A metal rhinestone joiner is used to hang the rhinestone charm to the front of the jar. You can also use a large jewelry split ring to hang the charm from the narrow ribbon.

JAR CONTENTS

1. Use the same ribbons and the adhesive backed rhinestone trim to decorate the glass vials. Create your own printed labels to decorate the vials. Fill the vials with bath salts or sugar scrubs using some of the recipes on page 77. Vials should hold just enough salts for one bath.

2. Repackage small gift soaps with rice paper. Add ribbon, rhinestones and printed labels.

3. Here are some ideas for other items that you may find to fill the jar: Small containers of travel creams and soap gels can be found at most drugstores. Save cosmetic samples to use as gifts. Drugstores also carry items such as small sea sponges, nail brushes, bath oil beads, body scrubbers, and many more spa-like items.

4. Place all items in the jar and pour in some decorative rhinestones to complete the presentation.

Jars pictured: at left, "Ombré Bath Salts Jar" and at right, "Spa in a Jar."

Ombré Bath Salts

Pamper Yourself

• YOU DESERVE IT •

Vanilla Rose Lotion

Ombré Bath Salts Jar

This jar makes a beautiful presentation for layered bath salts! Aromatic "salts de bain" are always appreciated. This decorated jar is so pretty the recipient will be tempted to display it in the bath or bedroom rather than use the bath salts. The recipe for creating the Ombré Bath Salts as well as recipes for other bath salt variations, and sugar scrubs are shown on the right.

Supplies

Pint size canning jar with flat metal seal and screw-on band

Lacey fabric

Glue gun and glue sticks

Decorative ribbons: several types needed such as gathered tulle ribbon and narrow velvet ribbon

Ribbon rosette

Vintage pearl brooch

Rhinestone charm with split ring

Small scoop

JAR DECORATION

1. Glue the metal seal into the screw-on band using hot glue. Allow this to dry.

2. Cover the top of the lid with a lace fabric circle, bringing it down over the edge of the band. Allow the glue to dry, and then trim edges of lace even with edge of band. Cover the rim of the metal band with the several layers of decorative ribbons using the glue gun and hot glue to attach each. Cover the top of the lid with the ribbon rosette. Glue or pin on the vintage brooch in the middle of the rosette.

3. A metal rhinestone joiner is used to hang the rhinestone charm to the front of the jar. You can also use a large jewelry split ring to hang the charm from the narrow ribbon.

Spa Recipes

BASIC BATH-SALTS RECIPE

Bath salts are easy to make as the ingredients can be found in grocery stores, drugstores, health-food stores, and craft shops. You simply mix a fixative (such as Epsom salts, rock salt, sea salt, or baking soda) with scent (essential oils or fragrance oils) and add optional food coloring. The equipment you need is probably already in your home kitchen.

$1\frac{1}{2}$ cups Epsom salts

$1\frac{1}{2}$ cups rock salt

Food coloring: 3 to 4 drops

Fragrance oils: 20 to 30 drops

Equipment: Glass or metal bowls for mixing, metal spoons for mixing and measuring, glass measuring cups, paper towels, a small bottle to help pack down the salts in the jar.

1. Mix the ingredients by placing them in a covered jar and shaking until blended.

2. When giving this mix as a gift, include a card with the "Using Bath Salts" information on page 77.

3. Fragrance Blends:

Daisy Fresh: 10 drops each lime, lemon, and lavender

Effervescent Floral: 10 drops each jasmine, lavender, and violet

Luscious Lily: 10 drops each lemongrass, orange, and lavender

Rose Dream: 15 drops each rose and vanilla

LAYERED OMBRÉ BATH-SALTS RECIPE

These layered bath salts are colored and scented in three batches.

1½ cups Epsom salts
1½ cups rock salt
Red food coloring
Fragrance oils of your choice

1. First layer: Mix ½ cup Epsom salts and ½ cup rock salt. Color with 4 drops red food coloring to make a dark pink. Scent with 15 drops fragrance oil. Mix well and pour into the jar, filling ⅓ of the jar.
2. Second layer: Mix ½ cup Epsom salts and ½ cup rock salt. Color with 2 drops red food coloring to make a light pink. Scent with 15 drops fragrance oil. Mix well and pour into jar until it is ⅔ full.
3. Third layer: ½ cup Epsom salts and ½ cup rock salt. No food coloring is added. Scent with 15 drops fragrance oil. Add this mix to fill the jar.
4. When giving this mix as a gift, include a card with the "Using Bath Salts" information to the right.

BASIC SUGAR-SCRUB RECIPE

The sugar scrub will keep for three months in a sealed container at room temperature. Sugar scrubs make great gifts and can be fragranced to match the bath salts for a lovely collection.

Makes 2¼ cups

½ cup oil (use coconut oil, almond oil, or safflower oil)
1½ cups sugar (use ultra fine white, white granulated, or brown sugar)
¼ cup honey
10 drops vitamin E oil
Fragrance oil, 20 to 30 drops

1. Combine the ingredients in a bowl. Stir until thoroughly combined.
2. Store in a sealed container for up to 3 months.
3. When giving this mix as a gift, include a card with the "Using Sugar Scrubs" information that follows.
4. Fragrance Blends:
Daisy Fresh: 10 drops each lime, lemon, and lavender
Effervescent Floral: 10 drops each jasmine, lavender, and violet
Luscious Lily: 10 drops each lemongrass, orange, and lavender
Rose Dream: 15 drops each rose and vanilla

USING BATH SALTS

Draw a warm bath and, as you fill the tub, add the fragrant salts to the running water. Hop in and relax, inhaling deeply to experience the refreshing and soothing aromas. The base of bath salts neutralizes the acids on your skin so the fragrance clings to the body. The scents are soothing, and the Epsom salts relax and heal your skin. Lying in a warm, scented bath transforms and renews your outlook; it's not just to get clean. A fragrant salt bath, with the flicker of candles surrounding, can become a refuge from the turmoil of modern everyday life, a luxury that is affordable to everyone.

USING SUGAR SCRUBS

Apply sugar scrub to wet skin. Gently massage the scrub into skin to polish and refresh. Rinse skin with warm water. Towel dry.

Forest Bird Jar

Give this jar as a gift to a nature lover or keep it for yourself as a room accent. This jar holds a forest-inspired scene with a cheerful bird and has a rustic matching lid. When creating the jar, a pair of chopsticks are handy for placing items into the bottom of the jar.

Supplies

Pint canning jar with flat metal seal and screw-on band

Preserved moss

Mushroom bird

Other natural items like twigs, acorns, lichen, etc.

Silicone-based glue

Acrylic enamel metal paints: copper and pale turquoise

Sponge applicator

Sea sponge

Burlap fabric

Pencil

Scissors

Light turquoise rickrack

Glue gun and glue sticks

Chopsticks

INSIDE JAR

1. Glue the moss into the bottom of the jar with the silicone glue.

2. Glue the bird and the other natural materials into the inside of the jar using dots of silicone glue on the items.

JAR LID

1. Paint the band with turquoise paint. Allow to dry. Using the sea sponge, lightly sponge the band with copper paint. Allow to dry, allowing some of the turquoise paint to show through. Let dry.

2. Use the metal seal as a template to cut a circle from burlap fabric. Cover the top of the lid with this circle of burlap, gluing in place with the glue gun.

3. Glue the rickrack trim to the rim of the band using the glue gun.

4. Place a bead of hot glue around the top inside of the metal band. Quickly and carefully place the metal seal into the band. Immediately attach the lid tightly to jar while glue is drying.

Fairy Mushroom Jar

This terrarium look-alike jar was painted on the inside using sparkle acrylic enamel paint for a magical view of a fairy mushroom scene.

Supplies

Pint canning jar with flat metal seal and screw-on band

Acrylic enamel paint: clear sparkle

Acrylic enamel clear medium

Serrated knife

Plastic foam ball

Glue gun and glue sticks

Preserved moss

Twigs

Mushrooms: variety of sizes (The large mushroom is a wooden cabinet knob painted with acrylic paints.)

INSTRUCTIONS

1. Coat the inside of the jar with sparkle acrylic enamel paint that has been thinned to a pourable consistency with clear medium. See basic painting instructions in the "Painted Jars" chapter for information on painting inside of jars. Let dry.

2. Using a serrated knife, cut the plastic foam ball in half.

3. Glue the flat metal ring into the band using the glue gun.

4. Build your scene inside the lid, occasionally checking that it will fit into the jar. To start, glue the half plastic foam ball into the lid. This will raise the scene allowing it to be better situated in the jar. Glue the moss to cover the plastic foam ball with dots of hot glue. Arrange the mushrooms and twigs and glue to secure. Glue a little moss on the twigs for added accent.

5. Place the jar on top of the lid and screw closed. Optional: Tiny battery operated lights would look awesome in this jar producing a magical night-light.

Christmas Trees Snow Globe

This wonderland-like snow globe, with lots of sparkly movement, makes a picturesque holiday display and a great teacher gift! These globes are so easy and fun to make, your children will love creating their own. Making them is a great activity for kids' parties, allowing the guests to leave with a snow globe party favor.

Supplies

Recycled jars with lids, or pint jars with tight fitting lids. Choose jars with little or no embossing to create snow globes with the clearest view.

Hot glue gun with clear glue sticks

Small display items such as bottlebrush trees and plastic deer. Choose plastic or ceramic items that will not rust for the best results. If you do have metal items, spray with clear oil-based varnish to prevent rusting.

Mylar glitter, or large flake nonmetal glitter

Distilled water

Glycerin

Silicone-based adhesive

JAR DECORATION

1. Glue the items for the scene into the jar lid using the glue gun and let dry. You will want to build a very sturdy base so the items do not come loose when you shake the jar. Next, add an extra layer of glue, and then sprinkle with glitter to cover while glue is still wet. Let dry.

2. Measure out the amount of water needed to fill the jar. Mix the water with a few drops glycerin. Mix well. The glycerin will make the water viscous, allowing the glitter to fall more slowly. Fill the jar with this water mixture, leaving a small ¼" gap at the top.

3. Screw the lid on, turn it right side up and shake. Evaluate the amount of glitter and add more if needed. When you are satisfied with the glitter, glue on the lid with the silicone based adhesive for a permanently closed and sealed snow globe.

Picnic for the Birds

Fill this jar with birdseed as a charming gift for a gardener or bird lover. Layer the birdseed (hulled and unhulled sunflower seeds, chick corn, millet, thistle, raw peanuts) for an attractive filler.

Supplies

Narrow mouth quart canning jar with flat metal seal and screw-on band (A recycled jar would also work well.)

Glue gun and glue sticks

Preserved moss

Small plastic egg

Musical note fabric ribbon, ⅝" width

Matching card stock tag or card stock to cut your own tag

Bird charm

Twine

LID DECORATION

1. Place a bead of hot glue around the top inside of the metal band. Place the metal seal and permanently glue the band in place.

2. Make a nest on top of lid with small bits of moss glued on with the glue gun. Glue the egg in the nest.

3. Glue the ribbon around the rim of the lid using the glue gun with small dots of glue.

4. Make a gift tag from decorative card stock or use a premade tag. Glue the bird charm in place on the tag.

5. Wrap twine around the neck of the jar and add the gift tag.

Knobs on Jars

Use fancy cabinet knobs to quickly dress up plain jars! Different methods allow a wide variety of knobs to be used on the jars.

CLEAR-BLUE KNOB

This design features a glass knob with the added element of a glass bead. Drill a hole into the center of the lid to accommodate the screw shaft of the knob. Thread a bead onto the screw shaft and then the grommet washer. Place the screw shaft into the hole on the lid from the top. Add a washer and nut to the underside of the lid to hold tight. If your knob is on a break-off screw, you can shorten the screw area showing in the jar by breaking it with a wire cutter.

CERAMIC FLORAL KNOB

The ceramic flower is actually a fancy pushpin (with the pin snapped off) that was glued onto a knob base with silicone adhesive. The knob base was then glued onto the lid with the silicone adhesive.

BEACH-GLASS KNOB

Large beach glass stones are found in the floral department of craft stores. This one was simply glued onto a knob with a flat top. Drill a hole into the center of the lid to accommodate a short metal screw. Place the screw into the hole to attach.

Ruffled Paper Jar Tops

This is a very simple and quick way to add a pretty ruffle to the jar tops. Fill the jars with homemade candy treats or a cupcake! I found that three liners are the maximum number you can add before they start to interfere with the band fastening easily. When using jars as gifts, fill them with your favorite mixes and include a recipe card for the mixes. These jars contain chocolate treats. See the "Culinary Gifts" chapter for recipes.

Supplies

Pint canning jar with flat metal seal and screw-on band.

Cupcake liner papers: 3 per jar

Strong adhesive tape runner or multi glue (You will need a glue that is thin and has a permanent hold.)

LID DECORATION

1. The paper liners are not quite large enough in diameter to cover the lids and also allow excess for a ruffle. Therefore I did some adjusting. First cut two of the cupcake liners in half to produce four halves.

2. Apply a strip of the adhesive tape runner or multi glue to the underside of each liner piece, along the cut edge. Attach two of the 1/2 liner pieces to the flat metal lid edge, opposite one another. Turn the lid 90 degrees and attach the remaining two pieces.

3. Place a whole liner paper on top of the lid covering the top, place the lid on the jar and screw on the band.

Blackboard Lids

These reusable lids are very handy for labeling containers or adding a decorative touch to a jar filled with a culinary gift. Painted with blackboard paint, chalk can be used to label the lid, then wiped off later to add a different label. Use a white paint pen if you wish the label to be permanent.

Supplies

Flat metal seal and screw-on band
Strong adhesive tape runner
Scrap of cardboard
Chalkboard acrylic enamel paint
Sponge applicator
Chalk pencil or paint pen: white

LID DECORATION

1. With the strong adhesive tape, attach the flat seal to the cardboard. This makes painting and handling the lid much easier.
2. Basecoat the lid with the blackboard paint. Let dry. Remove from cardboard and remove adhesive from underside of lid.
3. For lettering, use a white chalk pencil for a removable label or a white paint pen for a permanent label.

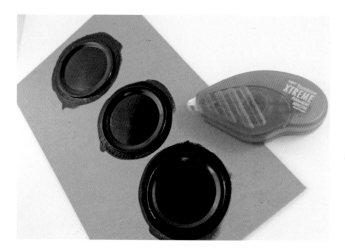

Blackboard paint was used to make a label for a personalized jar. See the "Chalkboard Label Jars" project in the "Painted Jars" chapter for the instructions and pattern for creating the label on the jar. In the "Culinary Gifts" chapter, you will find recipes for "Salads in a Jar."

Yarn Saver

This is a great gift to give a teenager as a way to introduce the joys of knitting or crocheting. It's also a great place to store a ball of yarn or twine of your own! An appreciated gift would be to fill the jar with a skein of yarn, a crochet hook, and instructions for making a crocheted dishcloth.

Supplies

Quart canning jar with metal seal and screw-on band

Drill with bit to fit grommet size

Grommet with washer (size to accommodate thicker wool or thinner twine)

Grommet setting tool

Hammer

Wool, crochet hook, and crochet pattern

INSTRUCTIONS

1. Using the drill bit, drill a hole in the flat seal lid. The hole should be slightly larger than the center hole of the grommet, and the grommet should fit in snugly. Make this hole in the center of the lid.

2. Follow the manufacturer's directions to set the grommet and washer into the lid.

3. Reassemble the seal and band. Place the wool inside and thread the end through the hole. Screw lid onto jar.

Drinking Jars

Here is a creative and easy way to give a gift of a personalized mug. Or make them for your next party so that guests can use them and then take them home as a party favor. Dress them up with tape name tags and colorful straws to match any party décor.

Supplies

Pint canning jars with handles and flat metal seals with screw-on bands

Drill with ¼" bit

Grommets, 1" size with washers—the inner hole large enough to fit paper straw (I found grommets in the fabric department packaged with a setting tool.)

Grommet setting tool

Small hammer

Washi tape (strong paper tape with adhesive back that comes in patterns and various colors)

Permanent marker: black

INSTRUCTIONS

1. Clean and remove any lettering on the flat seal.

2. Using the drill and large ¼" bit, drill a hole in the flat seal lid. The hole should be slightly larger than the center hole of the grommet, and the grommet should fit in snugly. Make this hole to one side of the lid, making sure there is enough space for the grommet to lie flat. The hole at the side makes the drinking jar more comfortable to use.

3. Follow the manufacturer's instructions to set the grommet and washer into the lid.

4. Reassemble the lid onto the jar.

5. Make a washi tape name tag for the front. Add the name with a black marker.

Soap-Dispenser Jar

When your plastic soap dispenser is empty and the bottle looks bad but the pump still works, there is a way to recycle the pump. Use it to make a new soap dispenser from a canning jar. Or you can purchase a new bottle of soap in a plastic jar to use. Metal pumps are also available for purchase to create your soap dispenser. The methods for using the plastic or metal pumps are very different. I have included the instructions for using either. Choose the method that fits with the type of pump you are using.

TECHNIQUE FOR USING CLEAR PLASTIC BOTTLE & PUMP

Supplies

Pint canning jar with flat metal seal and screw-on band

Recycled clear plastic soap bottle with pump or a new soap pump

Craft knife

Permanent marker: black

Hammer

Large nail

Scrap piece of wood

Wire cutters

INSTRUCTIONS

1. If you are using a new plastic dispenser, twist off the pump and pour the liquid soap into the canning jar. Set aside.

2. Wash and dry the plastic bottle you are using. With a craft knife, carefully cut off the top of the plastic bottle, leaving approximately 1" of the shoulder of the bottle attached. You will use this top piece and discard the remainder of the bottle.

3. Trace around the top opening of the plastic bottle piece into the very center of the flat seal with the marker to mark the size of hole you will need to make.

4. With the flat seal on a piece of wood, hammer the nail around the traced circle, keeping the nail holes very close together. You will use this perforation as a cutting guide and a starter for making the hole easier to cut. Using the wire cutters, cut out the center of the circle along the nail holes.

5. Fill the jar with soap. Push the plastic bottle piece into the hole of the lid, pushing the bottle up from the under side of the seal. Place this lid assembly onto the jar and screw on the metal band. Screw the pump onto the mouth of the plastic bottle piece.

TECHNIQUE FOR USING METAL PUMP

Supplies

Pint canning jar with flat metal seal and screw-on band

Metal pump (These can be found in the bathroom and kitchen décor departments.)

Permanent marker: black

Hammer

Large nail

Scrap piece of wood

Wire cutters

INSTRUCTIONS

1. Measure the top of the pump tubing piece to determine the size of circle you will need to cut in the lid in order to thread the metal part of the pump through the hole with a snug fit. Draw this circle size onto the top of the flat seal using the marker.

2. With the flat seal on a piece of wood, hammer the nail around the traced circle, keeping the nail holes very close together. You will use this perforation as a cutting guide and a starter for making the hole easier to cut. Using the wire cutters, cut out the center of the circle along the nail holes.

3. Fill the jar with liquid soap. Place the pump into the hole and reassemble the lid onto the jar.

1

2

3

1. Use a nail to perforate the lid where the hole is to be cut.
2. Cut out the hole to accommodate the bottle top using wire cutters.
3. Insert the plastic bottle top into lid.

Design-Punched Lids

A gift of fragrance is always received warmly. Using glass jars that have metal lids with holes helps distribute the scent from dried botanicals or layered potpourri while attractively displaying the collections of dried botanicals. Fill the plain jars with your favorite potpourri or your own homemade potpourri blends. Recipes for potpourri blends follow.

Supplies

Jar with a flat metal seal and screw-on band

Tracing paper

Pencil

Low-tack masking tape

Hammer

Awl

Scrap piece of wood

INSTRUCTIONS

1. Trace the design onto a piece of paper. Tape the paper to the top of the lid.

2. Place the lid on the wood and, using an awl and a hammer, lightly tap in the holes. You can adjust the size of the holes easily by tapping harder to make bigger holes. Be careful not to hammer too hard as the lid could warp.

3. Add a label that says, "Do not Consume."

LAYERED OCEAN POTPOURRI

Simply layer the dried botanicals in the jar, packing down after each layer, and add fragrance to the top layer of botanicals. This is a beautiful clean-smelling potpourri.

Oak moss

Whole blue juniper berries

Small white clamshells

Blue larkspur flowers

White snail shells

Fragrance oils: 20 drops peppermint and 20 drops lavender

Small bottle or muddling tool for tamping

1. Layer the ingredients in 1" layers using the order given. Pack down each layer before adding next layer by tamping.

2. Repeat until jar is full, and use the snail shells as the last layer, filling the jar to the top.

3. Pour the fragrance onto the top layer.

4. Add a lid with punched holes and screw on the band.

LAVENDER-FIELDS POTPOURRI

Oak moss

Pink rosebuds

Rosemary leaves

Blue juniper berries

Fragrance oils: 20 drops lavender and 10 drops rose

Small bottle or muddling tool for tamping

1. Place a layer of Oak moss in the bottom of the jar and then the next three ingredients in 1″ layers in the order given. Pack down each layer before adding next layer.

2. Use additional oak moss to fill the jar to the top.

3. Pour the fragrance onto the top layer.

4. Add a lid with punched holes and screw on the lid.

COFFEE-SCENTED POTPOURRI

Carob bean pods

Natural milo berries

Coffee beans

Cinnamon sticks in 1″ pieces

Natural milo berries

Coffee beans

Whole allspice berries

Fragrance oils: 20 drops chocolate and 20 drops espresso

Small bottle or muddling tool for tamping

1. Layer the ingredients in 1″ layers in the order given. Pack down each layer before adding next layer.

2. Pour the fragrance onto the top layer.

3. Add a lid with punched holes and screw on the band.

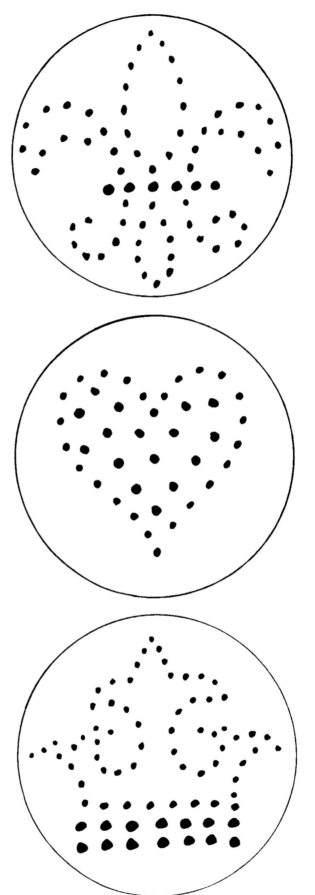

Labels & Tags

Labels and tags add interest to jars, convey useful information and are a lovely way to further personalize a gift. Label your gift to identify the recipient or the contents of a jar; provide instructions or recipes for how to use what is in the jar; or add a greeting. A little touch like a label or a tag makes the gift personal and heartfelt.

You'll find a wide variety of blank or preprinted, self-adhesive labels for decorating jars, lids, and gift tags at craft and art supply shops, department stores, and office-supply marts. Before applying labels to your jars, make sure your jar surface is clean and grease-free. Some labels may need to wrap around the jar and stick to themselves to prevent the label from pulling away from the jar.

You can make your own labels and tags from just about any kind of paper. This is a great way of using left over bits and pieces of special papers. Simply cut out an attractive shape and write the sentiment with a colorful marker. When designing your tags and labels, carry over the theme of the jar design by decorating them with the same materials that you used to decorate the lid or jar. Attach them to the jar or use ribbon, cord, or raffia tied around the neck of the jar to hang them.

A home computer is so convenient for designing and printing custom labels. Add photographs and design motifs on double-sided adhesive paper or with a laminating machine. The machine is especially handy if you're making and decorating lots of jars for gifts or to sell. With all the fonts, design motifs, and photos available online, there will be no end to your creativity.

BASIC SUPPLIES FOR TAGS & LABELS

Papers: card stock, decorative paper

Trims and embellishments: stickers, self-adhesive labels, ribbon, elastic cord, raffia, beads

Decorative-edge scissors

Tag dies and die cutter

Hole punches

Markers or gel pens

Glue gun and clear glue sticks

LABEL & TAG TIPS

- A tag die and die cutter machine is great for cutting out tags from decorative paper–you can make lots of tags easily.
- When using lightweight decorative paper for a tag, glue it to a piece of heavier card stock.
- Use decorative-edge scissors to cut interesting edges on layered paper panels.

- Write greetings and lettering with gel pens or felt pens.
- Use a variety of hole punch shapes and eyelets on your tag or label so that you can attach them to jars with elastic cord or ribbon.
- When you take the time to create a decorated jar of layered cookie or soup mix, make sure you give the same attention to labeling the jar's contents and including instructions or recipes so the recipient will know how to use the contents.
- You can handwrite your labels and recipes, or you can design and print them out on a computer using card stock.
- Paint, stencils, rubber stamps, and charms are other ways to decorate your labels and tags.
- If you're making lots of jars for gifts, you may wish to create a page of decorated labels or cards and have them duplicated on a color copier.
- Laminating recipe cards with laminating film or using a laminating machine is a practical touch.

Culinary Gifts

TECHNIQUES AND RECIPES

Culinary gifts in decorated jars are a way to share a favorite recipe. They give the recipient three gifts in one—the gift of something delicious to eat, the gift of the jar, and the gift of your time.

My recipes come from many sources—my family, my friends, and my adaptations of personal favorites. All the recipes have been tested in my kitchen and approved by the critical taste-testings of family members. I tried to make the recipes both traditional and unique, so the idea is familiar and appealing, but the gift is one that cannot be bought in a store. Each mix given here comes with a recipe or two for making the mix into something yummy.

If you have a favorite recipe, don't hesitate to put the mix in a jar and share it with a friend. Making your own mixes saves money and gives the opportunity to reduce preservatives, additives, salt, and sugar in the finished product. When giving the mixes as a gift, be sure to include a recipe card, laminated for an extra practical touch, and a list of all the ingredients used in the mix in case of allergies. Make the jar embellishments for culinary gifts practical ones. A gingerbread man cookie cutter attached to a jar of gingerbread cookie mix or a tea ball on a jar of tea will make the gift much more special.

The jars used to contain the cornbread mix and soup mix are featured in the "Cozy Jar Collection" project found in the "Quick Tricks" chapter.

TECHNIQUES FOR PREPARING AND USING JARS

STERILIZING JARS

The glass jars you use to package food gifts should be sterilized before use.

1. Check all jars for chips and cracks. If chipped or cracked, don't use for food. Check lids for dents or rust. If dented or rusty, don't use for food.

2. Wash all parts with hot, soapy water. Rinse.

3. To sterilize jars, place on a rack in large pot and cover with water. Let water come to a boil and boil for 15 minutes. Remove and dry completely before filling. Option: sterilize jars and lids in the dishwasher.

BASIC EQUIPMENT FOR FILLING JARS

Wooden spoons for mixing

Large spoon for filling jars

Small bottle or muddler with a flat bottom for tamping down the ingredients as you layer or place them in the jar

Paper towels for cleaning up as you go and wiping powdery ingredients off jars

A canning funnel (available at stores where canning supplies are sold) or a piece of card stock to make a simple funnel for filling the jars

TIPS FOR FILLING JARS

Culinary mixes often look better when the ingredients for the mix are layered in the jar. The recipient can mix the ingredients before using them. Layer ingredients in the jar in the order given in the recipe.

For a better appearance, wipe down the inside unfilled area of the jar with a clean paper towel after adding powdery ingredients, such as powdered (icing) sugar, cocoa, or flour, before adding the next ingredient.

Pack down all ingredients firmly. If you don't, you won't have enough space to fit in all the ingredients. (You will be surprised at how flour packs down!)

Generally, a quart jar holds 6 cups of packed down ingredients; a pint jar holds 3 cups of packed down ingredients. This is, however, a very general observation, as each recipe is made up of different ingredients that all pack down differently. If your ingredients do not come to the top of the jar, fill with crumpled plastic wrap or wax paper to prevent the ingredients from shifting and mixing.

STORING CULINARY MIXES

Cool, dry storage is best. Never store finished jars near a heat source, hot pipes, stove, or furnace or in direct sunlight. If you cannot guarantee cool and dry storage, it's better to store your mixes in the refrigerator.

One excellent quality of your homemade mixes is that they are preservative-free. For maximum freshness, label them with a "best before" date. Many factors determine the "best before" date, such as the type of flour (all-purpose flour has a longer shelf life than whole-wheat flour), preserving method (freshly dried herbs from your garden verses dried herbs bought from a market), and the general quality and freshness of the ingredients you use. These factors have been taken in account when suggesting these recommended best-before dates:

- Dressing, dip, and seasoning blends: 6 months
- Beans, dried vegetable soup blends: 3 months
- Bread, muffin, and scone mixes: 2 weeks in the refrigerator
- Cookie and cake mixes: 2 months; with nuts: 1 month
- Coffee and tea mixes: 3 months

Even though many mixes would last much longer than the suggested times, the strength of the colors and flavors will fade. The goal is to provide foods that are both safe and of high quality. Remember quality is not the same as safety. A poor-quality food (such as stale cereal) may be safe to eat; an unsafe food may look and taste good but contain harmful bacteria.

RECIPES

I have included recipes that can be used to fill the jars. Also included are recipes for the mixes to make cookies, bread, soups, etc. If you wish, you can photocopy these recipes, adhere them to card stock or other sturdy decorative paper, and give them along with your mixes in a jar.

Salads in a Jar

Gift your office mates with their own labeled jars for bringing food to work for lunch. Everyone at the office will know who is eating a delicious healthy lunch when a salad is stored in a personalized jar. Lunchtime salads are easy to assemble in a pint or quart jar for a fresh, healthy meal. Partner this personalized jar with a jar of salad dressing mix for a very special treat. Overnight oatmeal in a jar as well as a yogurt parfait in a jar are also great for transporting.

The following salad recipes can be adjusted by adding more or less of some ingredients and even by adding some ingredients not listed that are favorites. Following the layering steps will help to keep everything crisp and fresh. Be sure to chop all the ingredients into bite-size pieces.

1. First layer of ingredients in the bottom of the jar is the premixed salad dressing.

2. Second layer is hard vegetables such as carrots, celery, sweet peppers, red onion, cucumber, broccoli, or cauliflower.

3. Next is the soft vegetable layer such as tomatoes, green onions, corn, or avocado.

4. Add a protein layer by using one or more of the following: cheese, cooked meats, beans, or hard-boiled eggs.

5. The greens come next: lettuce, spinach, kale, or arugula.

6. Top the salad off with crunchy ingredients such as bacon bits, croutons, or roasted nuts and seeds.

7. Keeps salads in the refrigerator until ready to eat. Do not keep longer than 36 hours. Before eating, shake to coat the ingredients with dressing.

COLORFUL CAPRESE SALAD RECIPE

Use the best quality mozzarella cheese and the freshest tomatoes for this classic salad!

1 serving

LAYER AS FOLLOWS:

Dressing: 1 tablespoon balsamic vinegar and 2 tablespoons extra virgin olive oil

Single layer mini fresh mozzarella cheese balls

Chopped red tomato

Two fresh basil leaves

Another layer of mozzarella cheese balls

Chopped yellow tomato

Top with two more basil leaves

GREEK SALAD RECIPE

A favorite recipe that keeps well for a few days in the refrigerator.

1 serving

LAYER AS FOLLOWS:

Dressing: 1 tablespoon red wine vinegar, 2 tablespoons extra virgin olive oil, chopped fresh oregano

Chopped yellow sweet pepper

Chopped cucumber

Red cherry tomatoes cut in half

Crumbled feta cheese

Chopped spinach or lettuce

Here is a personalized jar that is perfect for bringing lunch to the office. No one will mistake it for his or her lunch. Blackboard paint creates a label on the jar for personalization and on the lid of the jar that holds salad dressing herb mix. See the project "Chalkboard Label Jars" in the "Painted Jars" chapter for instructions to create the jar. See the following pages for recipes to create salads in a jar and herbal mixes for dressings.

COBB SALAD RECIPE

1 serving

LAYER AS FOLLOWS:

Dressing: 2 tablespoon ranch dressing

Chopped tomato

Chopped green onion

Chopped avocado

Chopped cooked chicken breast

1 hard-boiled egg, sliced

Crumbled blue cheese

Chopped lettuce

Top with crumbled bacon

TACO SALAD RECIPE

1 serving

LAYER AS FOLLOWS:

Dressing: 1 tablespoon Catalina dressing and
1 tablespoon salsa

Chopped tomatoes

Cooked and cooled corn kernels

Black beans

Ground meat cooked with taco seasoning

Shredded cheddar cheese

Chopped iceberg lettuce

Chopped green onion

OVERNIGHT OATMEAL RECIPE

Pint jar with lid

$1/3$ cup rolled oats (not instant)

$1/2$ cup milk (or almond milk)

Cinnamon to taste

2 tablespoons dried fruit (cranberries, chopped apricots, or raisins)

1 tablespoon honey

1. Mix all the ingredients. Spoon mix into the jar. Place the lid on and refrigerate overnight.
2. Eat the oatmeal cold or place in the microwave for a few minutes for a warm breakfast.

YOGURT PARFAIT IN A JAR

Pint jar with lid

$1/2$ cup vanilla Greek yogurt

$1/2$ cup granola

Fresh blueberries and raspberries

1. Spoon a $1/4$ cup of yogurt into the jar.
2. Next add a $1/4$ cup layer of granola.
3. Top this layer with fresh blueberries and raspberries.
4. Repeat steps 1–3 one more time.

Herb-and-Spice Blends as Gifts

Herb-and-spice blends are easy to put together, yet are so essential for the home cook. They can be used for seasoning meats and vegetables, making salad dressings, and more. Included here are several blends with recipes to go with them. It is best to blend the seasonings before putting in the jar, rather than layering them.

HERBES DE PROVENCE HERB BLEND

Makes ½ cup

2 tablespoons marjoram

2 tablespoons dried oregano

1 tablespoon dried rosemary

1 tablespoon dried thyme

2 teaspoons dried lavender buds

2 teaspoons dried fennel seeds

1. Blend ingredients and package in a small sterilized jar.
2. Include the "French Country-Fried Fish Recipe" when giving this herb blend as a gift. Add the "best before" date of six months to your labeling information.

FRENCH COUNTRY-FRIED FISH RECIPE

Serves 4

1 tablespoon Herbes de Provence mix

2 cups dried breadcrumbs

1 pound white fish fillets such as halibut, cod, or haddock

1 egg, beaten

2 tablespoons vegetable oil

1. Mix the herb blend and the crumbs together and place on wax paper.
2. Dip the fish pieces in egg, then in the crumb mixture to coat both sides of fillets. Shake off excess.
3. Heat the oil in a heavy frying pan on medium/high heat. Fry the fish until golden on both sides and the fish flakes easily with a fork.

The jar used to contain these herbs is featured in the "Italian Countryside" project found in the "Decoupage and Trimmed Jars" chapter.

LEMON-DILL HERB BLEND

Makes ½ cup

4 tablespoons dried parsley

2 tablespoons dried dill

1 tablespoon dried lemon peel

1 tablespoon dried garlic granules

1. Blend all ingredients and package in a small sterilized jar.

2. Include the "Grilled Lemon-Dill Chicken Recipe" when giving this herb blend as a gift. Add the "best before" date of six months to your labeling information.

GRILLED LEMON-DILL CHICKEN RECIPE

Serves 4

1 tablespoon Lemon Dill Herb Blend

¼ cup fresh lemon juice

¼ cup olive oil

6 chicken breasts

1. In a shallow dish, stir together Lemon Dill Herb Blend, lemon juice, and oil.

2. Add the chicken breasts and marinate in the refrigerator for 1 hour.

3. Grill over hot coals or under the broiler for approximately 10 minutes per side until no longer pink and juices run clear.

MEDITERRANEAN HERB BLEND

Makes ¾ cup

3 tablespoons sun-dried tomatoes

2 tablespoons dried basil

2 tablespoons dried parsley

1 tablespoon dried oregano

½ tablespoon dried garlic granules

½ tablespoon dried lemon peel

1 teaspoon dried red pepper flakes

1. Blend all ingredients and package in a small sterilized jar.

2. Include the "Mediterranean Herb Vinaigrette Recipe" when giving this herb blend as a gift. Add the "best before" date of six months to your labeling information.

MEDITERRANEAN HERB VINAIGRETTE RECIPE

1 tablespoon Mediterranean Herb Blend

¼ cup olive oil

Juice of one lemon

1. Mix all ingredients.

2. Refrigerate for a few hours to allow the flavors to blend.

3. Stir to mix well before pouring on salad greens or grilled vegetables.

RANCH DRESSING MIX

Makes ¼ cup

1½ tablespoons dried parsley

1 tablespoon salt

½ tablespoon dried chives

¼ tablespoon dried oregano

¼ tablespoon dried tarragon

½ tablespoon garlic powder

½ tablespoon lemon pepper

1. Blend all ingredients and package in a small sterilized jar.
2. Include the "Ranch Dressing Recipe" and the "Ranch Dip Recipe" when giving this herb blend as a gift. Add the "best before" date of six months to your labeling information.

RANCH DRESSING RECIPE

Makes 1 cup

1 tablespoon Ranch Dressing Mix or Dilly Ranch Dressing Mix

½ cup mayonnaise

½ cup buttermilk

Whisk all ingredients together in a bowl. Refrigerate for 1 hour before serving.

DILLY RANCH DRESSING MIX

Makes ¼ cup

1 tablespoon dried dill weed

1½ tablespoons dried parsley

1 teaspoon dried garlic granules

2 teaspoons dried onion flakes

2 teaspoons salt

½ teaspoon pepper

1. Blend all ingredients and package in a small sterilized jar.
2. Include the "Ranch Dressing Recipe" and the "Ranch Dip Recipe" when giving this herb blend as a gift. Add the "best before" date of six months to your labeling information.

RANCH DIP RECIPE

Makes 2 cups

2 tablespoons Ranch Dressing Mix or Dilly Ranch Dressing Mix

1 cup mayonnaise

1 cup sour cream or plain Greek yogurt

Combine all ingredients in a bowl. Refrigerate for 2 hours. Serve as a dip for raw vegetables or as a topping for baked potatoes.

Soup Mixes as Gifts

Your gift of a jar of soup mix will be sincerely appreciated on a cold winter day when all that is needed to make a warming pot of soup is the gift mix, some water, and a few fresh ingredients. You've done all the work of gathering and combining. Now your friend can relax, enjoy the fruits of your labor, and take in the aroma.

TUSCAN MARKET SOUP MIX

$\frac{1}{2}$ cup barley

$\frac{1}{2}$ cup split peas

$\frac{1}{2}$ cup rice

$\frac{1}{2}$ cup lentils

2 tablespoons dried minced onion

2 tablespoons dried parsley

2 teaspoons salt

$\frac{1}{2}$ teaspoon pepper

2 tablespoons beef bouillon granules

1 teaspoon dried cumin

1 package dehydrated onion soup mix

1. Layer ingredients in a sterilized quart jar.
2. Include the "Tuscan Market Soup Recipe" when giving this mix as a gift. Add the "best before" date of three months to your labeling information.

COMFORT SOUP MIX

$\frac{1}{2}$ cup pearl barley

$\frac{1}{2}$ cup red beans

$\frac{1}{2}$ cup baby lima beans

$\frac{1}{2}$ cup split peas

$\frac{1}{2}$ cup pinto beans

$\frac{1}{2}$ cup black-eyed peas

$\frac{1}{2}$ cup yellow split peas

$\frac{1}{2}$ cup navy beans

$\frac{1}{2}$ cup green or brown lentils

1. Layer the ingredients in a sterilized quart jar.
2. Include the "Comfort Soup Recipe" when giving this mix as a gift. Add the "best before" date of three months to your labeling information.

LENTIL SOUP MIX

1 cup green lentils

1 cup red lentils

3 chicken bouillon cubes, crumbed

$\frac{1}{2}$ teaspoon dried thyme

1 teaspoon garlic powder

$\frac{1}{2}$ teaspoon salt

1. Mix all ingredients and package in a sterilized pint jar.
2. Include the "Lentil Soup Recipe" when giving the mix as a gift. Add the "best before" date of three months to your labeling information.

The jar used to contain the soup mix is featured in the "Italian Countryside" project found in the "Decoupage and Trimmed Jars" chapter.

COMFORT
Bean Soup Mix
1 Jar Comfort Bean Soup Mix
2 quarts water
1 ham hock
1 1/4 teaspoons salt
1 teaspoon pepper
1 can (28 oz.) diced tomatoes
1 large onion, chopped
1 garlic clove, minced

Place bean soup mix in a bowl. Add 2 quarts water and soak overnight. Drain. Bring 2 quarts water to boil in a soup pot. Add ham hock and simmer 20 minutes. Remove ham hock, cut meat from bone, chop and add back into pot. Add drained, soaked beans and remaining ingredients. Bring to boil, reduce heat and simmer 1 hour.

SPLIT PEA SOUP MIX

Makes 3 cups

2 cups green split peas
½ cup red lentils
½ cup yellow split peas
2 teaspoons salt
½ teaspoon pepper
1 teaspoon dried thyme
1 dried bay leaf

1. Layer the peas and the lentils in a sterilized glass quart jar.
2. Add the seasonings on top. Slip the bay leaf between the peas and the side of the jar.
3. Include the "Split Pea Soup Recipe" when giving this mix as a gift. Add the "best before" date of three months to your labeling information.

LENTIL NOODLE SOUP MIX

¼ cup red lentils
2 tablespoons dried minced onion
1½ tablespoons chicken bouillon granules
½ teaspoon dill
⅛ teaspoon celery seed
⅛ teaspoon garlic powder
1 bay leaf
1 cup uncooked egg noodles

1. Layer ingredients in a pint sterilized glass jar.
2. Include the "Lentil Turkey Noodle Soup Recipe" when giving this mix as a gift. Add the "best before" date of three months to your labeling information.

TUSCAN MARKET SOUP RECIPE

Serves 8–10

1 jar Tuscan Market Soup Mix
3 quarts water
2 stalks celery, chopped
2 carrots, sliced
1 cup shredded cabbage
1 can (28 oz.) crushed tomatoes

1. Combine all ingredients and place in soup pot. Cover.
2. Bring to a boil. Turn heat down so soup is just simmering. Cook 1 hour or until vegetables are tender.

COMFORT SOUP RECIPE

Serves 6–8

1 jar Comfort Soup Mix
2 quarts water
1 ham hock
1¼ teaspoons salt
1 teaspoon pepper
1 can (28 oz.) diced tomatoes
1 large onion, chopped
1 garlic glove, minced

1. Place soup mix in a pot or bowl. Add 2 quarts of water and soak overnight. Drain.
2. Bring 2 quarts of water to a boil in a soup pot. Add ham hock and simmer 20 minutes. Remove ham hock.
3. Add soaked and drained bean soup mix and remaining ingredients.
4. Bring to a boil. Turn heat down so soup is just simmering. Cook 1 hour or until vegetables are tender.

LENTIL SOUP RECIPE

Serves 6-8

1 jar Lentil Soup Mix
2 quarts water
2 carrots, peeled and chopped
2 stalks celery, chopped
1/2 cup chopped onions
Red pepper sauce

1. In a large stockpot, combine Lentil Soup Mix and water.
2. Bring to a boil and add vegetables. Bring up to a boil again. Partially cover pot. Turn heat down to a simmer and cook for 1 hour or until lentils are soft.
3. Add a splash of red pepper sauce to the pot before serving.

LENTIL TURKEY NOODLE SOUP RECIPE

Serves 6-8

1 jar Lentil Noodle Soup Mix
2 tablespoons vegetable oil
1 medium onion, chopped
3 carrots, peeled and chopped
3 stalks celery, chopped
8 cups water
2 cups cooked turkey

1. Heat the oil in a large stockpot. Add the onion, carrots, and celery. Sauté until the vegetables are tender.
2. Add the Lentil Noodle Soup Mix and the water to the pot. Bring to a boil. Add cooked turkey. Reduce to a simmer and cook until noodles and lentils are done.

SPLIT PEA SOUP RECIPE

Serves 8

1 jar Split Pea Soup Mix
2 tablespoons vegetable oil
1 medium onion, chopped
3 carrots, peeled and chopped
3 stalks celery, chopped
1 pound Polish or other sausage, sliced 1/2" thick
2 1/2 quarts water

1. Heat the oil in a large stockpot. Add the onion, carrots, celery, and sausage. Sauté until the vegetables are tender.
2. Add the Split Pea Soup Mix and the water to the pot. Bring to a boil. Reduce to a simmer. Cook for 2-3 hours or until vegetables are tender.

Bread Mixes as Gifts

Nothing smells better than baking bread—and your gift makes a loaf of warm bread easy to achieve. These bread recipes are so good you may want to keep some of the mix for yourself.

HERB BEER BREAD MIX

2²/₃ cups flour

2 tablespoons sugar

2 tablespoons baking powder

1 teaspoon salt

1 teaspoon dried oregano

1 teaspoon dried thyme

¹/₂ teaspoon dried dill

1. Blend ingredients together. Place in a sterilized pint jar.

2. Include the "Herb Beer Bread Recipe" or the "Cheesy Beer Bread Recipe" when giving this mix as a gift. If you like, you could also include a can of beer. Add the "best before" date of two weeks in refrigerator to your labeling information.

HERB BEER BREAD RECIPE

Makes 1 loaf

1 jar Herb Beer Bread Mix

12 oz. can of beer (or sparkling water)

¼ cup melted butter

1. Grease a loaf pan. Preheat the oven to 375 degrees F.

2. In a large bowl, combine the Herb Beer Bread Mix with the can of beer or sparkling water. Stir until just moist.

3. Place the batter in the prepared pan. Bake for 45–50 minutes. Remove from the oven and brush with melted butter.

CHEESY BEER BREAD RECIPE

Makes 1 loaf

1 jar Herb Beer Bread Mix

1 cup grated cheddar cheese

12 oz. can beer (or sparkling water)

¼ cup melted butter

1. Grease a loaf pan. Preheat the oven to 375 degrees F.

2. In a large bowl, combine the Herb Beer Bread Mix and grated cheese. Add the can of beer or sparkling water. Stir until just moist.

3. Place the batter in the prepared pan. Bake for 45 to 50 minutes. Remove from the oven and brush with melted butter.

COMFORT CORNBREAD MIX

1 cup flour

2 cups yellow cornmeal

⅓ cup sugar

4 teaspoons baking powder

1 teaspoon salt

1. Layer in a pint sterilized glass jar.

2. Include the "Comfort Cornbread Recipe" when giving this mix as a gift. Add the "best before" date of two weeks in refrigerator to your labeling information.

COMFORT CORNBREAD RECIPE

1 jar Cornbread Mix

1 egg

1 cup milk

⅓ cup melted butter

1. Preheat oven to 400 degrees F.

2. Blend mix in a large bowl. Mix egg, milk, and butter and add to dry mixture. Stir only until moistened.

3. Pour into greased loaf pan or muffin tin and bake 20–25 minutes. Serve hot with butter.

Drink Mixes as Gifts

Here you will find recipes for tea blends, mulling spices, as well as some instant coffee and cocoa drinks. When you give a mix as a gift, don't forget to include the recipes and the "best by" dates recommended for each blend. Teas and herbs lose their potency and colors fade after several months.

FAVORITE TEA BLEND

Makes ⅓ cup

1 teaspoon dried lemon verbena leaves

1 teaspoon dried peppermint leaves

1 teaspoon dried rose hips

1 teaspoon dried hibiscus flowers

3 tablespoons orange pekoe tea

1. Combine ingredients and package in a small jar. Increase the recipe to fill a larger jar.

2. Include the recipe for "A Perfect Pot of Tea" when giving this mix as a gift. Add the "best before" date of three months to your labeling information.

A PERFECT POT OF TEA

Makes 1 pot of tea

1. Warm a 6-cup teapot with a cup of boiling water. Discard the water.

2. Place the package of Favorite Blend Tea Mix (⅓ cup) in the teapot. Heat water in a kettle and when at a full boil, pour over the tea mix.

3. Let steep for 3 minutes for weak tea and no longer than 6 minutes for strong tea.

4. Serve with cream, sugar, or lemon, if desired.

CHAI SPICE MIX

This makes a warming, spicy cup of tea. It takes a bit more effort to prepare but is well worth the effort. A jar of chai spices is an excellent present for the more adventurous people on your gift list. Tie a small tea strainer (sieve) to the jar to add to the presentation.

Dried ginger pieces

Black peppercorns

Cinnamon sticks, broken into small pieces

Whole cardamom pods

Whole cloves

Whole coriander seed pods

1. Layer ingredients in equal portions in a sterilized jar, using the size jar you desire.

2. Include the "Authentic Indian Chai Tea Recipe" when giving this mix as a gift. Add the "best before" date of three months to your labeling information.

The jar used to contain the cocoa mix is featured in the "Globe Jar Top" project found in the "Quick Tricks" chapter.

The jar used to contain the spiced mocha coffee mix is featured in the "Blackboard Lids" project found in the "Quick Tricks" chapter.

SPICED MOCHA COFFEE MIX

⅓ cup instant coffee

½ cup cocoa

½ cup nonfat dry milk

1 teaspoon ground cinnamon

2 teaspoons dried orange peel

1. Layer the ingredients in a half-pint sterilized glass jar.

2. Include the "Spiced Mocha Coffee Recipe" when giving this mix as a gift. You could also present it with a bar of chocolate and cinnamon sticks. Add the "best before" date of three months to your labeling information.

SPICED MOCHA COFFEE RECIPE

Makes 1 serving

1 tablespoon Spiced Mocha Coffee Mix

6 ounces boiling water

Shaved chocolate

Cinnamon stick

Place the coffee mix in the bottom of a coffee mug. Pour in boiling water. Stir to mix. Garnish with shaved chocolate and a cinnamon stick.

AUTHENTIC INDIAN CHAI TEA RECIPE

Makes 3 cups

1 tablespoon Chai Spice Mix

1 heapingtablespoon black tea

1 cup whole milk (or soy or rice milk)

Sugar to taste

1. Blend the Chai Spice Mix to distribute spices evenly throughout. Place 1 tablespoon of Chai Spice Mix in a saucepan with 3 cups water.

2. Simmer the spice and water for 10 minutes. Remove from heat.

3. Add the black tea. Let steep 5 minutes.

4. While the tea is steeping, warm the milk until steaming but not boiling. Strain the tea and spice mixture through a sieve into the milk. Sweeten to taste with sugar.

MULLED CRANBERRY MIX

Makes 1½ cups

10 cinnamon sticks, broken
⅓ cup whole cloves
⅓ cup whole allspice
2 tablespoons dried orange peel
½ cup dried cranberries

1. Combine all ingredients.
2. Package ¼ cup of the mix in a piece of cheesecloth. Tie with kitchen twine.
3. Fill a jar with cheesecloth packages of drink mix.
4. Include the "Mulled Cranberry Cider Recipe" when giving this mix as a gift. Add the "best before" date of three months to your labeling information.

MULLED CRANBERRY CIDER RECIPE

Makes 2 quarts

1 package (¼ cup) Mulled Cranberry Mix
1 quart apple cider
1 quart water
2 fresh oranges, sliced
½ pint dark rum (optional)

1. In a large saucepan, combine the cider, water, rum (if desired), and Mulled Cranberry Mix. Heat through, but do not boil. Add the orange slices from one orange and let steep 1 minute.
2. Serve warm, garnished with an orange slice.

HOT COCOA MIX

3 cups powdered milk
5 oz. package non-instant chocolate pudding mix
½ cup powdered nondairy creamer
¼ cup unsweetened cocoa powder
¼ cup superfine sugar
Mini marshmallows

1. Layer the first five ingredients in a quart canning jar in the order given. Fill the jar to the top with mini marshmallows.
2. Include the "Cup of Cocoa Recipe" when giving this mix as a gift. Add the "best before" date of three months to your labeling information.

CUP OF COCOA RECIPE

Make 1 cup

1 tablespoon Hot Cocoa Mix
1 cup of boiling water

1. Take the mini marshmallows from jar and keep them separate, storing in a resealable baggie or container.
2. Mix the hot cocoa mix to evenly distribute all the ingredients.
3. Add 1 tablespoon of the mix to the boiling water and stir. Add mini marshmallows to the top. Enjoy!

Cakes-in-a-Jar Gifts

Cake-in-a-Jar is a baked, ready-to-eat cake that is stored and baked in its container—the jar! (Basically, you are canning a cake.) The cakes last several months without refrigeration when processed correctly and are fun to give as gifts. Wide-mouth, pint canning jars with two-part lids (seal and screw-on band) are best for Cake-in-a-Jar. The cake can slide easily out after the jar is opened. I also use standard-mouth jars and offer the cakes with a spoon so the cake can be eaten right from the jar.

This batter is a bit thicker than regular cake batter, and the finished cakes are a little denser. Don't be afraid to experiment with the basic recipe or adjust your favorite cake recipes to make in jars. Each recipe makes 6 to 7 jar cakes.

CAKE-IN-A-JAR RECIPE

Pint canning jar for each cake

New metal flat lids with screw-on bands

$2^2/_3$ cup sugar

1 cup butter

4 eggs

$^1/_2$ cup water

2 teaspoons vanilla

$3^1/_2$ cups flour

1 teaspoon baking powder

$1^1/_2$ teaspoons baking soda

1 teaspoon salt

1. Preheat the oven to 325 degrees F.

2. Sterilize jars and seals. (You must use new seals.) Let the jars dry. Grease the bottoms and sides of the jars well with butter. Do not use spray oils to grease the jars.

3. Cream sugar and butter. Add eggs and mix well. Add water and vanilla. Mix the dry ingredients together and sift into the wet ingredients. Mix enough just to combine.

4. Pour 1 cup batter into each pint jar. Don't use more than that amount. If you do, the cake could overflow as it rises. Wipe the tops of the jars well with a clean, damp paper towel. The jar tops need to be clean; if they are not, you will not get a tight seal later.

5. Place the jars on a baking sheet, making sure the jars don't touch one another. Bake for 55–60 minutes. Check if the cake is done by inserting a wooden skewer. The cake is cooked when the skewer comes out clean. **NOTE:** The jars are very hot after baking. Remove from oven with care, using oven mitts on both hands.

6. Place seals on jars immediately after the cakes are removed from the oven. Screw on bands firmly, but not too tight. Let cool completely. Check to see that jars have sealed properly. The lid will be indented when sealed properly. Tighten the bands on the jars.

7. Cakes in jars that do not seal properly should be placed in the refrigerator and can be enjoyed by your family, or the jars can be frozen. Use properly sealed jars two months from baking as the "best before" date. If keeping longer, store the cakes in the refrigerator.

8. When giving these as gifts, be sure to include the "best before" date of two months on the label or tag that you make for the cake.

POLKA-DOT CAKE-IN-A-JAR VARIATION

Basic Cake-in-a-Jar recipe

1 cup mini candy-coated chocolate candies (M&Ms)

Mix and bake according to instructions for Basic Cake-in-a-Jar Recipe.

BANANA NUT CAKE VARIATION

Basic Cake-in-a-Jar recipe

2 cups mashed bananas

1 teaspoon cinnamon

²/₃ cup chopped pecans

Mix and bake according to instructions for Basic Cake-in-a-Jar Recipe.

ORANGE—POPPY-SEED CAKE VARIATION

Basic Cake-in-a-Jar recipe minus the water

1 cup white chocolate pieces

¼ cup poppy seeds

1 tablespoon fresh grated orange rind

½ cup orange juice

Mix and bake according to instructions for Basic Cake-in-a-Jar Recipe.

CHOCOLATE-ALMOND CAKE VARIATION

Basic Cake-in-a-Jar Recipe minus the water and vanilla

½ cup almond-flavored liqueur

2 cups semisweet chocolate pieces

1 cup almonds

Mix and bake according to instructions for Basic Cake-in-a-Jar Recipe.

RUM-RAISIN CAKE VARIATION

Basic Cake-in-a-Jar Recipe minus the water

½ cup dark rum

1 cup raisins

Mix and bake according to instructions for Basic Cake-in-a-Jar Recipe.

Cookie-Mix Gifts

BEST-EVER COOKIE MIX

2½ cups flour

1 teaspoon baking soda

1 teaspoon salt

1 cup brown sugar

½ cup fine granulated sugar

1 cup chopped pecans or walnuts

1 cup mini candy-coated chocolate pieces

1. Sift together the flour with the baking soda and salt.

2. Layer the flour mixture, sugars, nuts, and candies in a sterilized glass quart jar.

3. Include the "Best-Ever Cookie Recipe" when giving this mix as a gift. Add the "best before" date of one month to your labeling information.

BEST-EVER COOKIE RECIPE
Makes 4 dozen

1 jar Best-Ever Cookie Mix

1 cup butter, softened

2 eggs

2 teaspoons vanilla extract

1. Preheat the oven to 375 degrees F.

2. Using an electric mixer, cream the butter, eggs, and vanilla together.

3. Add the cookie mix and stir until well blended.

4. Drop the cookies by rounded tablespoonfuls on an ungreased cookie sheet. Bake for 8–10 minutes, until golden brown. Transfer to a wire rack to cool.

CHOCOLATE BROWNIE MIX

Makes 5½ cups of mix

2 cups sugar

1 cup cocoa powder

1 cup all-purpose flour

1 cup chopped pecans

½ cup chocolate chips

1. Layer the ingredients in a quart-size sterilized glass jar.

2. Include the "Chocolate Brownie Recipe" when giving this mix as a gift. Add the "best before" date of one month to your labeling information.

CHOCOLATE-GINGERBREAD COOKIE MIX

2½ cups all-purpose flour

⅔ cup sugar

1½ cups semi-sweet chocolate pieces

¼ teaspoon salt

½ teaspoon baking soda

1 teaspoon ground ginger

¼ teaspoon ground nutmeg

1. Sift the ingredients together. Place in a quart sterilized glass jar.

2. Include the "Chocolate-Gingerbread Folks Recipe" when giving this mix as a gift. Add the "best before" date of two months to your labeling information.

GINGER SCONE MIX

This is not an attractive-looking mix and can't be layered, so it's best presented in an opaque, painted jar.

3 cups all purpose flour

1 cup buttermilk powder

1½ tablespoon baking powder

½ tablespoon cream of tartar

1 teaspoon salt

¾ cup brown sugar

½ cup shortening

½ cup candied ginger, finely chopped

1. Sift the first five ingredients together. Add the brown sugar and mix thoroughly to combine.

2. Cut the shortening into the dry ingredients with a pastry cutter until the mixture resembles fine crumbs. Add the candied ginger.

3. Divide into 2-cup portions. Package each portion in a pint jar.

4. Include the "Ginger Scones Recipe" when giving this mix as a gift. Add the "best before" date of two weeks in the refrigerator to your labeling information.

CHOCOLATE BROWNIE RECIPE
Makes 24

1 jar Chocolate Brownie Mix

1 cup butter

4 eggs

1. Preheat the oven to 325 degrees F. Grease and flour a 13" x 9" pan.

2. Using an electric mixer, cream the butter. Add the eggs one at a time, beating well after each addition.

3. Add the brownie mix and continue to mix by hand until smooth.

4. Spread the mixture into the prepared pan. Bake 40–50 minutes until a wooden skewer comes out clean.

OATMEAL-TOFFEE COOKIE MIX

1½ cups all-purpose flour

1 teaspoon baking soda

1 teaspoon cinnamon

1 cup brown sugar

⅓ cup granulated sugar

2 chocolate-covered toffee candy bars, coarsely chopped

3 cups rolled oats

1. Sift together the flour, baking soda, and cinnamon.

2. Layer the flour mixture and all the other ingredients in a sterilized glass quart jar.

3. Include the "Oatmeal-Toffee Cookie Recipe" when giving this mix as a gift. Add the "best before" date of two months to your labeling information.

CHOCOLATE-GINGERBREAD FOLKS RECIPE

Makes about 2 dozen cookies

1 jar Chocolate-Gingerbread Cookie Mix

1/2 cup molasses

1/2 cup butter

1/4 cup hot water

1. Preheat the oven to 375 degrees F.
2. Place a sieve on a mixing bowl. Pour mix through sieve to remove chocolate pieces.
3. Combine molasses, butter, and chocolate pieces in a double boiler and heat until chocolate is melted. Stir until smooth. Stir in hot water. Add dry ingredients and mix well. Chill in refrigerator until firm (about 2 hours).
4. Cut the dough in four pieces of equal size. On a floured board, working with one piece of dough at a time, roll the dough to a 1/4" thickness. Using a cookie cutter, cut into gingerbread man shapes.
5. Place cookies on an ungreased cookie sheet. Bake for 8–10 minutes. Cool on a rack. Repeat with the remaining dough.

GINGER SCONES RECIPE

Makes 12 scones

2 cups (1 jar) Candied Ginger Scone Mix

1 egg

1/3 cup light cream

1. Preheat the oven to 400 degrees F. Place the scone mix in a large bowl.
2. Lightly beat the egg. Add it to the mix. Add the cream. Stir until mixture forms a ball. Be careful not to overmix.
3. Turn the dough out on a lightly floured surface and pat to a 3/4" thickness. Form the dough either into a circle or a square. Cut the dough in 12 wedges or square pieces of equal size.
4. Arrange 2" apart on an ungreased baking sheet. Bake for 10–15 minutes until lightly browned.

OATMEAL-TOFFEE COOKIE RECIPE
Makes 4 dozen cookies

1 jar Oatmeal-Toffee Cookie Mix

1 1/4 cups butter

1 egg

1 teaspoon vanilla

1. Preheat the oven to 375 degrees F.
2. Using an electric mixer, cream the butter, egg, and vanilla together.
3. Add the cookie mix. Stir until well blended.
4. Drop the cookies by rounded tablespoonfuls on ungreased cookie sheets. Bake 8–10 minutes, until golden brown. Transfer to a wire rack to cool.

Homemade Treat Gifts

Gather your family together for a fun day of making treats for your friends and neighbors. The recipes are easy enough so that kids can join in the fun.

CANDIED POPCORN RECIPE

Make this recipe to fill a quart jar with this yummy treat.

2 cups sugar

2 cups light brown sugar, firmly packed

2 cups light cream

1 teaspoon soft butter

3/4 teaspoon vanilla

1/2 cup whole almonds or pecans

6 cups popped popcorn, with unpopped kernels removed

1. Combine sugars and cream. Stir until sugar is dissolved. Boil in a heavy bottomed saucepan uncovered without stirring until syrup reaches soft-ball stage (235–240 degrees F). Cool for 10 minutes.
2. Beat this mixture with a wooden spoon until thickened. Add butter and vanilla and mix in. Then add nuts and popcorn. Mix well to distribute syrup.
3. Pour on sheets of parchment paper to cool. Break apart larger pieces and package in airtight jars.

SUGAR 'N SPICE NUTS RECIPE

This sweet-and-spicy blend of nuts will be a welcomed gift when packaged in a beautifully decorated jar.

1/2 cup brown sugar

1/2 cup sugar

1 teaspoon cinnamon

1/2 teaspoon ginger

1/2 teaspoon nutmeg

1 egg white

1 tablespoon water

I teaspoon vanilla

4 cups pecans or mixed nuts

1. Combine sugars and spices. Beat egg white, water, and vanilla until frothy. Add sugar and spice mixture to egg whites. Add nuts and mix to coat all nuts.
2. Spread on greased baking sheet and bake in the oven at 325 degrees F for 20 minutes, stirring occasionally. The nuts should look dry and slightly browned.
3. Allow to cool before adding to a dry sterilized glass jar.

ROASTED NUTS RECIPE

This savory blend of nuts will nicely fill a pint size jar.

1 tablespoon butter

2 tablespoons ketchup

2 tablespoons Worcestershire sauce

1/4 teaspoon cayenne pepper

1/4 teaspoon garlic salt

2 cups whole pecans or almonds

1. Melt butter. Add ketchup, Worcestershire sauce, cayenne pepper, and garlic salt. Mix well.
2. Add nuts and stir until nuts are well-coated.
3. Spread on greased baking sheet. Bake in the oven at 350 degrees F for 20 minutes.
4. Allow to cool before adding to a dry sterilized glass jar.

The jars used to contain these chocolate treats are featured in the "Ruffled Paper Jar Tops" project found in the "Quick Tricks" chapter.

CHOCOLATE-DIPPED TREATS

Making chocolate-dipped treats is a very easy, fun activity for the whole family. Make the production of these tasty treats a holiday tradition in your home. Do this activity in cooler weather season for best results.

Ingredient Options

Baking chocolate or chocolate bars—use the best chocolate your budget will allow. Using good-quality chocolate (such as Belgian chocolate) makes all the difference in the finished product! You may use dark, milk, or white chocolate

Nuts such as toasted hazelnuts, almonds, or walnuts

Dried fruit such as raisins, cranberries, blueberries, apricots, or papaya spears

Candied popcorn

Mini pretzels (Add colorful candy sprinkles before chocolate sets up.)

1. Method #1 for melting chocolate: Place broken pieces of chocolate in a large heatproof bowl. Set this bowl over another bowl or pan of boiling water. Do not allow bowl with chocolate in to touch boiling water. Stir until smooth. DO NOT get any water in chocolate.
2. Method #2 for melting chocolate: Place chocolate in a large glass or ceramic heatproof dish. Melt in microwave in 15-second intervals, mixing between each.
3. Place the items to be dipped into the bowl of melted chocolate and quickly mix to coat. Remove pieces to a waxed paper, parchment, or foil-covered baking sheet with a slotted spoon or fork. Separate pieces so that there are no large clumps. Allow to cool and harden.
4. Do not store finished dipped products in the refrigerator. Store in an airtight sterilized glass jar.

CHOCOLATE TRUFFLES RECIPE

Makes approximately 70 truffles. This recipe works well for shipping during cold weather season.

2 cups semisweet chocolate chips

2 cups milk chocolate chips

$2/3$ cup whipping cream

2 teaspoons vanilla

Ground cocoa, toasted coconut, chopped nuts, or melted chocolate

1. Combine chocolate chips, cream, and vanilla in a saucepan. Heat and stir on low heat until chocolate chips melt and mixture is smooth. Remove from heat and cool to room temperature. Place in refrigerator and chill until firm.

2. Shape into balls, using 1 heaping teaspoon for each ball. Roll truffles in cocoa, toasted fine coconut, or chopped nuts. You could also dip them in melted chocolate. Another variation is to shape the truffle mixture over a single toasted hazelnut before rolling in cocoa.

3. Package in dry sterilized glass jars. Store in cool, dry area.

CANDIED PRETZELS RECIPE

1 package mini twist pretzels

2 cups nuts

1 cup unsalted butter

2 cups brown sugar

$1/2$ cup light corn syrup

Pinch salt

1. Preheat oven to 250 degrees F.

2. Combine pretzels and nuts in a heatproof large bowl. Set aside.

3. Combine butter, sugar, syrup, and salt. Bring to boil and cook until very thick. Pour sugar mixture over pretzels and nuts and lightly and quickly mix. Immediately place on a greased cookie sheet.

4. Bake in oven for 20 minutes, stirring after 10 minutes. Remove from oven and spread on wax paper to cool.

5. Package in a dry sterilized glass jar.

NUTS 'N BOLTS

This is my husband's favorite—we call this recipe "Scott's Legendary Nuts 'n Bolts." It has become a tradition for him to make this for everyone on our gift list. I get the job of decorating the jars.

1 tablespoon Worcestershire sauce

$1/2$ tablespoon garlic powder

1 tablespoon seasoning salt

1 cup peanut oil

3 cups round oat cereal

3 cups mini shredded wheat cereal

3 cups crispy squares cereal

2 cups pretzel sticks

2 lbs. salted mixed nuts

1. Preheat oven to 250 degrees F.

2. Mix the Worcestershire sauce, garlic powder, seasoning salt, and peanut oil in a bowl. Mix cereals and pretzel sticks in another bowl. Pour the spiced oil over the cereal mixture and stir to coat.

3. Pour onto a rimmed baking sheet. Bake for 2 hours, stirring every 15 minutes. Allow to cool.

4. Combine this cereal mix with the nuts in a large bowl.

5. Package in a dry sterilized glass jar.

Doggy Treats as Gifts

Use this mix and the "Doggy Treats Recipe" to make goodies for your favorite doggy friend. Or you could give this mix to a human friend who is an avid baker so he or she can bake fresh treats.

DOGGY TREATS MIX

1 cup whole wheat flour

1/2 cup powdered milk

1/2 cup soy bacon bits

1 teaspoon sea salt

1/8 cup sugar

1 tablespoon beef bouillon granules or powder

1. Layer the mix in a pint jar.

2. Include the "Doggy Treats Recipe" when giving this mix as a gift. Add the "best before" date of two months to your labeling information.

DOGGY TREATS RECIPE

1 pint jar Doggy Treats Mix

1/4 cup water

1 egg

Cookie cutter

1. Preheat oven to 400 degrees F.

2. Mix all ingredients in a bowl until moist and well mixed.

3. Turn mix out onto a board. Knead into dough. Roll dough out on a surface sprinkled with flour. Cut out shapes.

4. Bake for 30 minutes. Turn oven temperature to 200 degrees. Leave biscuits in oven to dry slowly until bone hard. Turn off oven and remove treats.

5. Package in a personalized jar.

The jar used to contain these doggy treats is featured in the "Good-Dog Goody Jar" project found in the "Painted Jars" chapter.

Index

A

Acrylic craft paints 10
Acrylic enamel paints 10, 12, 20, 22, 24, 26, 29, 30, 32, 33, 36, 54, 79
Acrylic glass paints 10
Acrylic paints for metal 36, 53, 78
Adhesive spray 20
Adhesive tabs 42, 46
Adhesive tape runners 42, 84, 86
Antique jars 8
Applicator(s) 13, 20, 26, 34, 53, 54, 78, 86
Authentic Indian Chai Tea Recipe 112
Awl 92

B

Baby wipes, see "wipes"
Ball jars 7
Basecoating 14
Bath salts 76, 77
Bath salts recipe 76
Batting 70
Beach-Glass Lanterns 34
Beachfront Property 54
Beads 64, 83, 94
Beer bread 108, 109
Best-Ever Cookie Mix 116
Best-Ever Cookie Recipe 116
Bird 78
Blackboard Lids 86, 112
Blackboard paint, see "Chalkboard paint"
Book page 48, 51
Book-Page Window Jar 48, 50
Book-Page Window-Jar patterns 50
Bread Mixes as Gifts 108, 109
Brownie 116
Brush(es) 13, 14, 20, 22, 24, 29, 30, 32, 33, 36, 42, 44, 46, 48, 51, 52, 58
Button(s) 53, 68, 72
Button Collection 53

C

Cake-in-a-Jar Recipe 114
Cake-in-a-Jar Gifts 114, 115
Candied Popcorn Recipe 120
Candied Pretzels Recipe 122
Canister 39
Canning jars 7, 8, 20, 22, 26, 32, 34, 36, 48, 53, 56, 58, 68, 72, 74, 76, 78, 79, 82, 84, 88, 89, 90, 92, 97, 114
Cardboard 86
Card stock 44, 46, 58, 82, 94
Chai Spice Mix 110, 112
Chai tea recipe 112
Chalkboard-Label Jars 26, 86, 98
Chalkboard paint 26, 86, 98
Charm 39, 56, 76, 82
Cheesy Beer-Bread Recipe 109
Chocolate Brownie Mix 116

Chocolate Brownie Recipe 117
Chocolate Dipped Treats 123
Chocolate-Gingerbread Cookie Mix 116
Chocolate-Gingerbread Folks Recipe 119
Chocolate Truffles Recipe 123
Christmas-Tree Snow Globe 80
Citrus Trio 36
Citrus-Trio Patterns 38
Clamps 34, 70
Clear medium, 20, 24, 79
Clothespins 68
Coasters 66, 67
Cobb Salad Recipe 100
Cocoa recipe 113
Coffee 93, 112
Coffee-Scented Potpourri 93
Coiled-Rope Coasters 66
Colorful Caprese Salad 98
Comfort Cornbread Mix 109
Comfort Cornbread Recipe 109
Comfort Soup Mix 104
Comfort Soup Recipe 106
Cookie Mix Gifts 116–119
Cork sheet 56, 66, 67, 73
Cotton swabs 13, 14
Cozy Jar Collection 68, 96
Craft knife 42, 46, 51, 52, 56, 66, 90
Culinary Gifts 39, 44, 46, 64, 68, 70, 84, 86, 96–125
Cup of Cocoa Recipe 113
Cupcake papers 84
Cutting 43
Cutting mat 42, 46, 51, 52, 56, 66

D

Decorative jars 8, 33
Decoupage 40, 43
Decoupage and Trimmed Jars 40–59, 101, 104
Decoupage medium 42, 44, 46, 48, 51, 52
Design Punched Lids 92, 93
Die-cutting machine 16, 56, 94
Dilly Ranch Dressing Mix 103
Dimensional paints 10, 12, 18, 29
Distressed Container Jars 33
Distressed Twine Jar 32
Distressing 10, 17, 32, 33
Doggie treats 39, 124
Doggie Treats as Gifts 124
Doggie Treats Recipe 124
Dots 10, 17
Drill 32, 88, 89
Drink Mixes as Gifts 110–113
Drinking Jars 89

E

Egg 82
Embroidery 72
Emery board 13, 17, 24, 32, 33
Enamel paints, see "acrylic enamel paints"

Etched glass 24, 34
Etched-Glass Apothecary Jars 24

F

Fabric 68, 70, 74, 76, 78
Fabric spray 66
Fabric-Topped Padded Lids 70
Fairy Mushroom Jar 79
Faux-Antique Milk Glass 28
Faux Mercury Glass 19, 24
Favorite Tea Blend 44, 110
Felt 62, 63
Fiberfill 72, 73
Forest Bird Jar 78
Freezer paper 13, 20, 26, 42, 44, 46, 48, 51, 52, 58, 66
French Country-Fried Fish Recipe 101
Fruit Sewing Kits 60, 62
Funnel 97

G

Gifts 6
Gilded Label Jar 58
Ginger Scone Mix 118
Ginger Scones Recipe 119
Gingerbread 116, 119
Glitter 64, 80
Globe Jar Top 64
Glue gun 42, 53, 62, 64, 70, 72, 73, 74, 76, 78, 79, 80, 82, 94
Glycerin 80
Good-Dog Goodie Jar 39, 124
Gravel 54
Greek Salad Recipe 98
Grilled Lemon-Dill Chicken Recipe 102
Grommet setting tool 32, 88, 89
Grommets 32, 88, 89

H

Hammer 32, 88, 89, 90, 92
Handmade papers 43, 74
Hemp 33
Herb and Spice Blends as Gifts 101–103
Herb Beer Bread Mix 108
Herb Beer Bread Recipe 109
Herbe de Provence Herb Blend 101
Hobnail 10, 18
Homemade Treat Gifts 120–123
Honey Jar 56
Hook-and-loop tabs 68
Hot Cocoa Mix 113

I

Italian Countryside 46, 101, 104

J

Jute 26, 44

K

Kerr jars 7
Knife 62, 79
Knobs on Jars 83

L

Labels & Tags 94
Lavender-Fields Potpourri 93
Layered-Ocean Potpourri 93
Lemon-Dill Chicken Recipe 102
Lemon-Dill Herb Blend 102
Lentil-Noodle Soup Mix 106
Lentil Soup Mix 104
Lentil Soup Recipe 107
Lentil Turkey Noodle Soup Recipe 107
Lids 9, 66, 67, 68, 70, 73, 86, 92, 93
Linen 72, 73

M

Marker(s) 54, 89, 90, 94
Masking tape 13, 14, 15, 20, 22, 24, 26, 92
Mason jars 7, 8
Matboard 66
Measuring tape, see "tape measure"
Mediterranean Herb Blend 102
Mediterranean-Herb Vinaigrette Recipe 102
Mercury glass 19
Metal leaf 58
Metal ribbon 34, 70
Milk glass 28
Moss 78, 79, 82
Mulled Cranberry Cider Recipe 113
Mulled Cranberry Mix 113
Multi glue 26, 42, 58, 66, 67, 84
Mushrooms 79

N

Nail 90
Napkins 43, 44
Nuts 120, 122, 123
Nuts 'n Bolts 122

O

Oatmeal 100, 118, 119
Oatmeal-Toffee Cookie Mix 118
Oatmeal-Toffee Cookie Recipe 119
Of Eastern Influence 39, 51
Ombré Bath Salts Jar 74, 76
Ombré painting 10, 18
Overnight-Oatmeal Recipe 100

P

Paint pens 12, 17, 26, 30, 36, 39, 58, 86
Painted Jars 10–39, 98, 124
Painting techniques 14
Paisley Label Jar 30
Paper(s) 42, 94
Paper napkins, see "napkins"
Paper towels 14, 29, 30, 48, 52, 97
Patterns 38, 50
Pearls 53
Pencil 44, 46, 48, 51, 52, 56, 58, 66, 67, 68, 70, 72, 73, 78, 92

Picnic for the Birds 60, 82
Pincushion 62, 63, 72, 73
Pincushion Button Jar 72
Pins 63, 72
Plastic foam 62, 79
Play Money 52
Pliers 34, 70
Popcorn 120, 123
Potpourri 92, 93
Pretzels 122, 123

Q

Quick Tricks 60-94, 96, 112, 120

R

Raffia 51, 94
Ranch Dip Recipe 103
Ranch Dressing Mix 103
Ranch Dressing Recipe 103
Recipe(s) 96, 97, 98, 100, 101, 102, 103, 104, 106, 107, 108, 112, 113, 114, 115, 116, 118, 120, 122, 123, 124
Recycled jars 8, 30, 40, 51, 52, 54, 62, 64, 80, 90
Red, White, and Blue 20
Repositionable spray adhesive, see "spray adhesive"
Rhinestone 74, 76
Ribbon 40, 44, 46, 64, 68, 72, 74, 76, 82, 94
Rice paper 51, 74
Rickrack trim 62, 63, 78
Roasted Nuts Recipe 120
Rope 66
Rubber stamp 56, 67
Ruffled-Paper Jar Tops 84, 120
Ruler 42, 44, 46, 48, 51, 56, 68

S

Salad recipes 98, 100
Salads in a Jar 86, 98-100
Sanding block 13, 17, 32, 33, 44
Scissors 42, 44, 46, 48, 51, 58, 62, 64, 66, 67, 68, 70, 72, 73, 74, 78, 94
Scones 118
Sealing 43
Sewing needle 68, 70, 72, 73
Shells 54
Silicone-based adhesives 42, 46, 52, 53, 54, 56, 67, 70, 78, 80
Soap 74
Soap Dispenser Jar 90
Soup Mixes as Gifts 104–107
Spa in a Jar 74
Spiced-Mocha Coffee Mix 44, 112
Spiced-Mocha Coffee Recipe 112
Split-Pea Soup Mix 106
Split-Pea Soup Recipe 107
Sponge(s) 13, 14, 17, 18, 78
Spoons 97, 114
Spray adhesive 16, 20, 42, 56
Spray paint 12, 14, 19, 20, 24, 58
Stamped-Cork Jar Lid Coasters 67
Stars 20
Stencils 10, 16, 20, 24, 26
Stenciling 16,
Stickers 20, 94

Stripes 20
Stylus 13, 36
Sugar-and-Spice Nuts Recipe 120
Sugar scrub recipe 77
Surface preparation 14

T

Taco Salad Recipe 100
Tags 48, 54, 60, 68, 82, 94
Tape measure 44, 46, 48, 51, 62, 68, 70
Tea 110
Tea and Coffee Canisters 44
Tearing 43
Template 44, 46, 58
Thread 68, 70, 72, 73
Tissue 43
Tracing paper 29, 30, 36, 92
Transfer paper 13, 14, 36
Transferring 14
Transparent glass paints 12, 15, 34
Trims 94
Tuscan Market Soup Mix 104
Tuscan Market Soup Recipe 106
Twigs 78, 79
Twine 32, 51, 54, 68, 82

V

Vintage Lid Pincushions 73
Votive 20

W

Washi tape 89
Wax paper 13
Wet wipes, see "wipes"
Whimsical Blossoms 22
White glue 53, 54, 64
Wipes 13, 48, 52
Wire 34
Wire bail jars 8, 29, 44, 46
Wire cutters 90
Wood 90, 92

Y

Yarn Saver 88
Yogurt Parfait in a Jar 100

About the Author

Marie Browning is the consummate craft designer and writer. For over 25 years Marie has inspired countless crafters internationally with her vast knowledge of mediums, products, and techniques. She is the bestselling author of numerous craft books and has created designs for various consumer and industry magazines. In addition to her prolific craft design, Marie is a creative consultant, assisting manufacturers in developing innovative products and identifying new ways to market their products to the craft consumer. Marie currently works as the signature Designer for American Tombow.

Marie has taught classes, demonstrated at trade shows, and appeared on TV and online videos. Her professional expertise and vast knowledge of the craft industry, coupled with her warm and encouraging way of making anyone feel like he or she can be creative, makes Marie and her company, Marie Browning Creates™, a true asset to the growth of the creative industry. She lives, gardens and crafts on Vancouver Island in Canada. She and her husband Scott have three children: Katelyn, Lena, and Jonathan. Marie can be contacted at **www.mariebrowning.com.**

Acknowledgments

Marie Browning thanks the following manufacturers for their generous contributions of materials used in this book.

Alltrista Corporation
www.alltrista.com
Glass jars, canning jars, antique jar reproductions

American Tombow
www.tombowusa.com
MONO Multi Liquid Glue, Xtreme Power Tabs, Xtreme Adhesive

Daler-Rowney
www.daler-rowney.com
Simply Simmons Brushes

DecoArt, Inc
www.decoart.com
Americana Gloss Enamels and Glass Paints, DecoArt Glass Paint Markers, Decou-Page™ Decoupage medium

Krylon
www.krylon.com
Short Cuts® Spray Paints, Looking Glass Mirror Spray Paint

Plaid Enterprises
www.plaidonline.com
FolkArt Enamel Paints, FolkArt Enamel Mediums, Gallery Glass transparent glass paint and liquid leading, Martha Stewart Glass Paints, Royal Coat decoupage medium, and Mod Podge